Mrs. Hungerford

Peter's Wife

Vol. III

Mrs. Hungerford

Peter's Wife
Vol. III

ISBN/EAN: 9783337052935

Printed in Europe, USA, Canada, Australia, Japan

Cover: Foto ©ninafisch / pixelio.de

More available books at **www.hansebooks.com**

PETER'S WIFE.

A Novel.

BY

MRS. HUNGERFORD,

AUTHOR OF
"MOLLY BAWN," "APRIL'S LADY," "A MAD PRANK,"
"LADY PATTY," "NORA CREINA," ETC.

IN THREE VOLUMES.

VOL. III.

LONDON:
F. V. WHITE & CO.,
14, BEDFORD STREET, STRAND, W.C.
1894.

PRINTED BY
KELLY AND CO. LIMITED, 182, 183 AND 184, HIGH HOLBORN, W.C.,
AND MIDDLE MILL, KINGSTON-ON-THAMES.

CONTENTS.

		PAGE
Chapter	I.	1
,,	II.	11
,,	III.	23
,,	IV.	33
,,	V.	45
,,	VI.	51
,,	VII.	64
,,	VIII.	74
,,	IX.	84
,,	X.	95
,,	XI.	102
,,	XII.	114
,,	XIII.	127
,,	XIV.	136
,,	XV.	151
,,	XVI.	170
,,	XVII.	181
,,	XVIII.	196
,,	XIX.	204
,,	XX.	215
,,	XXI.	223
,,	XXII.	236

PETER'S WIFE.

PETER'S WIFE.

CHAPTER I.

"For this I'm tempest-toss'd,
A drifting skiff at most,
I dare the waves, risk cloud and rain,
I ever tempt my fate again,
Nor care if I be lost."

It is a few days later, and now well into the heart of August. The mornings are a little colder, the evenings yellower, and the asters are holding up their stiff heads in all the borders. In the long avenue the leaves are beginning to fall, not in battalions, but softly, unconsciously, now and then, and one by one —teaching, imperceptibly as it were, the great lesson of life—the sad lesson of Death.

Thursday has come and gone. The Thursday looked forward to by Nell with fears not to be controlled. Cecilia had met her the morning after that strange scene in that room, quite as usual, save for a little increased tenderness in her greeting—poor Cecilia, who hated to be at variance with anyone—who had not enough strength for a quarrel. There had been a touch of remorse in her kiss, that had made Nell catch her and hold her, feeling inclined to cry the while. But Cecilia had said nothing more about Philip's coming. Therefore, as Nell knew, he *was* coming. And Nell wondered hourly if Cecilia feared or cared—or gave a thought to it at all.

Cecilia *had* cared, however, and thought a great deal, and feared, perhaps, even more than Nell—but hers had been a glad terror. It was full of sweetness, of strange, unknown expectation, of the misery that fills the winecup of life. Mingled with her fear, was a mad joy that would not be kept down, that sent her singing with a sweet passion through the gardens in the late morning, until some vague misgiving rose to kill the song. But underneath these misgivings, these sharp little pangs that caught her heart as if a child's hand grasped it—the music ever lay.

At times she felt unnerved and dispirited,

and found a difficulty in being quite herself. There was a burden on her hard to lift, and her shoulders were of the dainty kind that sink easily beneath a load. It was at these times, that the fear closed in upon her. She was so seldom *sure* of herself, even in the lighter, more ordinary affairs of her life ; how then could she be sure now—now when Fate was rushing on her? But perhaps, it was this very distrust of herself, this terrible uncertainty as to what she might or might not do on imagined occasions, that gave a keen edge to the indescribable thrill of ecstasy that always shook her when she dwelt on Philip's coming.

If it had all been laid open to her—if she had known how things would go; how she would be able to receive him ; how it would be with him; how much control she could depend upon—if all things had been made clear to her ; she longed for all this—or thought she did—but in reality it was the doubt that fascinated her—though she spent her days telling herself that there was no doubt—none—none. Philip would come, and she would take his visit calmly, and she would be happy for a little while. That he would go some day, she knew too—somewhere down at the back of her mind, but she refused to drag this thought into the light. She never dwelt upon it. She was strictly Scriptural in some things—she certainly gave no thought to the morrow! To-day was sufficient for her. Her to-days had, up to this, been singularly void of evil.

The Thursday had come, and with it Philip, but for a day only!

Stairs was a persistent man, if not a strong one—and indeed it was impossible not to see that he was positively weak in some ways. He was at all events capable of being crushed beneath a love affair—of being driven by passion as a leaf by the wind, and so far unable to resist the dragging of his heart strings, that they led him whithersoever they listed—a pretty dance at most times—and in his case where honour should have barred the way.

Yet in spite of all this he was a gentleman, and it revolted his small remaining sense of right and wrong—to sleep beneath Peter Gaveston's roof, to hold a fair face to him, and to eat his bread.

When he left Cecilia on that last evening in the orchard, he had been full of his promise to her, and no doubt if he had been a stronger man—or a man with a few less grains of the cravings that honour demand—he would have held to that promise, though all Heaven and earth swore at him! but honour was still a landmark with him, and he was not built of such strong fibre as some.

He had left her full of his determination to do as she would have him do, but once gone from her—when the silent darkness of the wood had caught and enfolded him in its grand tranquility—when the fascination that might surely be called "glamour" of her presence, fell away from him, he woke with a start from his dream and knew he could not do this thing. He could not accept Peter Gaveston's invitation. He stopped short in the darkness of the wood and thought. He knew at all events that he ought to refuse it.

But how? All the small world of Bigley-on-Sea knew he was going to Gaveston Hall on the expiration of his visit to the McGregors. It had been discussed everywhere. And to refuse now, to leave so abruptly, would surely lead to comment that must come home to Cecilia. He had thought this out before, and had decided risking the comments, but now again he hesitates.

It was rather unfortunate that the McGregors had discussed so openly the fact of his going *from* them, to the Hall. But they *had* done so very openly, and pleasurably, and certainly without an *arrière pensée*. But then other people had discussed it too, *not* openly, and decidedly not so pleasantly.

Stairs was aware of all this, and felt that a problem had been thrown upon his shoulders very difficult of solution. Would it be better for Cecilia if he were to go now—or if he were to accept Gaveston's invitation for a day, and so have it out? What was the best plan for Cecilia—Cecilia was all his thought —which rendering of the difficulty would best wither that poison, that lay beneath the aspish tongues of the Bigley-on-Sea people?

There were more to be considered than the Bigley-on-Sea's, however. There was Gaveston. Stairs had never overcome that first feeling of respect for Peter that had entered into him when he saw Cecilia's husband. How was he to explain to Gaveston his change of front?

He went slowly through the wood thinking, suffering torture so acute, that it seemed to touch his body even as his mind. His body and his mind indeed were fighting a hard and cruel fight. Finally they came to a settlement. He drew himself up, pausing — thinking.

Yes, he will go — on Thursday — and on Wednesday he will leave by the evening mail, that goes at seven. That is settled. He feels quite strong again. It is settled; nothing shall undo it. On Wednesday evening at six-thirty he will bid her good-bye. There must be an end of it somewhere, and it shall be then. It will be an easy matter to get a telegram to-morrow telling him of a friend who is going abroad, and who wants him to go with him. Such telegrams, if rare, are not unheard of. He will explain this to the McGregors first; the McGregors who are always so sympathetic, and so—talkative.

For a man invalided home as he had been, it would seem the most natural thing in the world. He had been ill. He desired to travel in the south of Europe with a view to picking up the loose threads of vitality that still seemed wickedly anxious to slip through the loom.

The McGregors — kind souls — would at once see the advantage of his spending, for his health's sake, the remaining months of his leave abroad. They would explain to others —the busy tongues would cease.

And he—he would see her again. He did not say "alone." He refused to admit that hope even to himself, and for once was a hypocrite. He would see her for her own sake, to stop the mouths of the gossips. Once again—and then——

He drew a long breath and looked out to the ocean. He had gained a hill, and all the vast magnificent field of water was laid bare to him. It was quite clear—quite clear—like the future he has planned for himself, and terribly barren!

> "There's not a ship in sight;
> And as the sun goes under,
> Thick clouds conspire to cover
> The moon that shall rise yonder.
> Thou art alone, fond lover."

Then! Yes! it would be all over then.

He went home and wrote a note to be sent to Gaveston next day—he felt he was outraging all the tenets of society, but he *could* not write to Cecilia—to say that pressing business would prevent his stopping longer with him than from Thursday to Friday. And he so far satisfied his conscience as to reduce those days to their shortest span so far as *his* use of them was concerned. He would come to dinner on Thursday, he wrote, and was sorry to say he should have to leave by the seven train on Wednesday. He was so disappointed about the whole thing, but a friend of his was starting in a week for

Norway, and he had promised him some time since to go with him, and——

There were a good many "ands," all of them very plausible and all of them entirely outside the boundary of truth.

Gaveston received the note and showed it to Cecilia, who made no sign. She turned slowly aside without a word of comment, but no emotion was visible. Perhaps she did not believe in it, but she acted as if she did, and to Nell's overwhelming surprise, who had read the letter too, she organized a rather large luncheon party for the Friday that was to see his final departure. It seemed as if she too were determined to prevent any last words.

CHAPTER II.

"That's a valiant flea that dares eat his breakfast on the lip of a lion."

THE luncheon has gone off admirably. Cecilia indeed had been the life and soul of it. She had asked Mrs. Chance and Mrs. Cutforth-Boss amongst others, in spite of Nell's protests. To the girl she seemed to *court* their observation—to compel them to see all that there was to be seen, between her and Stairs. This might have arisen out of petulant desire to prove to them how little there really was—to stifle their gossip in their throats.

But if so, she threw herself away. Gossip is not so easily to be stifled. A little dying ember dropped as all fires drop them, springs to fuller life through the shock, and sets ablaze again the smouldering logs, and so the game goes on.

It was, perhaps, a little unfortunate that

Gaveston had told them all at luncheon, that he must run up to town by the three-thirty train, and that he could not be home until the eleven-fifteen. It was decidedly unfortunate that he had to go, but the business was very imperative. He had apologised to Stairs about it early in the morning, when the telegram that summoned him had arrived. The fact of his not being back to bid him good-bye, seemed so inhospitable. Stairs' train took him away at seven, so that there was really no chance of seeing him again. He was genuinely sorry—and he had not noticed the strange light that came into Stairs' eyes as he made his announcement.

The younger man had murmured something necessary, and had then turned abruptly away. There was a singing in his ears. . . . He would be able then to bid her good-bye alone—alone!

They are all in the drawing-room now, moving about or talking in little groups, whilst putting on their gloves preparatory to departure.

Mrs. Chance has glided up to Peter, her

most engaging expression on her face, her little hesitation somewhat accentuated.

"So you are really going up to town this evening?"

"Yes. Can I do anything for you?" asks Gaveston kindly.

"What a noble offer. I wish I could avail myself of it. No, I . . . was only wondering how you could tear yourself away from your wife. I have heard . . . is it true?—that you have never been separated from her since your marriage for an hour."

"I am afraid we all hear a great deal of nonsense at times," says Gaveston laughing. "I am not so devoted a husband as all that comes to, and I have no doubt my wife will be able to endure existence without me for a few hours."

"You really think that?" with the prettiest smile.

"I really do," with the good-natured air of a man who is determined not to be bored. Mrs. Chance always bores Peter, a fact of which she is well aware, and resents immensely.

"You are very modest," says she. "I

shouldn't wonder"—with downcast eyes—
"if you didn't quite understand her."

"Even if I don't," pleasantly, and looking over her head with a view to escape, " and if your surmise is true, that she will miss me, I should be rather glad to believe it. Absence, you know, is popularly supposed to make the heart grow fonder."

"Now that is conceit," says Mrs. Chance. "Such vanity," playfully, " ought to be taken down a little. It wants a corrective. I shall administer it! Do you know, I once heard your wife call you——"

She pauses, glancing at him quite charmingly—mischief in her eyes however.

"She never calls me," says Gaveston. " Watson does that!"

"What a silly joke! Shan't I administer the correction then?"

"By all means, but you will have to be quick, for I must catch my train. She called me——?"

"Ugly," says Mrs. Chance. "Wasn't that a flight on her part—wasn't it absurd? Of course she didn't mean it—how could she?

—but she did really! Now I"—archly—"felt it my duty to tell you that—to take you down a little bit, as I said."

"I'm afraid you haven't succeeded," says Gaveston, smiling imperturbably. "I am afraid you have defeated your own"—pausing, "*admirable* purpose. I feel, if possible, more vain than ever—a veritable peacock. The idea that my wife, even when engrossed with her guests, takes the trouble to remember me, fills me with a vanity not to be suppressed. It also delights me to know that the guest to whom she made her little confidence, should remember it so long and take such trouble to repeat it to me."

His smile is as easy as ever, as he bids her good-bye, and goes on to the others, but somehow she knows she has changed Gaveston's feeling, from kindly toleration to distinct dislike. This is not a pleasant reflection for one who is living on sufferance. The effect on Mrs. Chance, however, is not to make her moderate her transports in the way of malice, but to increase them.

As for Gaveston—he had taken it all very

lightly, very carelessly, but in the carriage on his way to the station, where there is no one near him to divert his thoughts, Bella's ill-meant words come back to him.

"Ugly!" Cecilia had called him ugly, and openly—to a big crowd apparently. . . . Pshaw! what nonsense! Of course that woman's talk was not to be depended on. She was chaffing him, no doubt, in her extremely vulgar fashion! And even if Cecilia *had* said it, it was only said in fun. Cecilia was always poking fun at people.

He put it in many lights, but Mrs. Chance, if she had only known it, had done her work. That word "ugly" went with him up to town and down again.

* * * * *

"Have you heard," says Mrs. Cutforth-Boss, seating herself angularly on a seat next Mrs. McGregor, "that Mr. Gaveston is going by the three-thirty train? In fact, there he is now, saying good-bye. Such a mistake on his part."

"A mistake?" questions Mrs. McGregor,

who, dear good woman, never thinks of sin. "To say good-bye? It certainly *does* break up a party. But——"

"Nonsense! It will probably break up his life!"

"Dear Mrs. Cutforth-Boss? Surely you say more than you mean."

The delicate, kindly, common-place face grows distressed.

"Not a single syllable," says Maria sternly. "He must be *mad* to go away like this, leaving no one to keep an eye upon her."

"But, my dear, why should an eye be kept upon her?" says Mrs. McGregor, who is charity itself—the grand charity that thinketh no evil. "I suppose you are speaking of that dear girl Nell, and I should certainly think Mr. Gaveston would be right in leaving her to the care of her sister. Mrs. Gaveston surely is a sufficient chaperone."

"It is Mrs. Gaveston to whom I am alluding," says Maria grimly. "It is she"— severely—"who, in my opinion, requires a chaperone. And now she is left without one. Her husband is going up to town on some ridiculous business, leaving that silly fribble of a wife of his, alone with her lover. As if his business was not *hers*."

"It seems to me," says Mrs. McGregor quietly, "that you don't quite understand. Philip Stairs is incapable of such conduct as you represent . . . . and even if he were, he is going away this evening by the seven o'clock train."

"Is he?" says Maria. She is evidently surprised. "Are you sure?"

"Absolutely! Believe me, my dear friend, there is nothing in this absurd scandal."

"Well, if he goes I'll agree with you," says Maria grimly. "In the meantime," with a levity very foreign, "*we* must go now." Her gloves are already drawn on, and she begins to button them.

Mrs. Chance, being shunted by Gaveston, had found her way to Nell, who is standing in one of the windows with Grant. Cecilia had mentioned Sir Stephen as a guest for this strange luncheon-party, but Nell had implored her to leave him out. She had not explained to Cecilia her reasons for refusing to have

him, and Cecilia had not asked. The truth
was that Nell wished to be left, as far as
possible, with as few distractions as might be
on this one day. Grant she could manage,
but Sir Stephen was always a little *en évidence;*
he was shrewder than Grant, too, she thought,
and she feared for Cecilia. Her heart, indeed,
was full of Cecilia! Who was there to look
after her except she, Nell? Peter was going—
Mickey was gone.

Mickey's going had been at once a relief
and a regret to Nell. When with her, she
felt she had a trusty companion, who would
stick to her and hers, through all storms and
troubles. The Irishman, if rough and a little
boisterous at times, was kind at heart, and
would have done all he could for those he
loved, when at their worst point. And she
was sure that he loved Cecilia and Cecilia's
husband. He would help them if here. Yet
for all that, relief lay in the fact that he was
not here. It would have been terrible to her
that Mickey should have been present when
Philip came—and during Philip's stay. But
Mickey had gone back to his home in Cork

three days ago, after a parting with Nell that he hoped was pathetic.

"So Mr. McNamara is really gone?" says Mrs. Chance, coming up to Nell and her brother. "Do you know I quite thought he was—a—a fixture!"

Mrs. Wilding, who is close to them, talking to Mr. Nobbs, smiles and moves a little bit away, taking her small companion with her.

"One could almost wish he was," says Nell gently. "He is such a very charming companion."

"Of course you miss him?"

"Very much indeed."

"I can quite understand his being delightful in little ways—but an Irishman—is an Irishman ever to be trusted?"

"A gentleman is always to be trusted."

"Do you think so? Now Mr. McNamara struck me as being a . . . . well—a little troublesome—a little unsure. Always talking, you know—always looking round corners, as it were!" (Poor Mickey! he had seen through *her*, and she knows it!)

"You mistake Mr. McNamara," says Nell

coldly. " He was the last person in the world to look round corners."

" Oh! as for that, I hardly meant *that*. At least, I did not mean what you mean, naughty girl!" She smiles sweetly, and taps Nell on the arm with the glove she is holding, preparatory to putting it on.

"What do I mean?" asks Nell haughtily.

"Ha! ha! we won't go into it," with an arch glance that maddens Nell still further. " What I was going to say was that, Mr. McNamara struck me as being clever . . . a little *too* clever, perhaps."

" I am afraid you have studied him in vain," says Nell. "It is an open secret that he missed his exam. for the army, and had to take an agency instead."

She moves away, shaking her head at Grant—who is boiling with indignation—to prevent his following her.

Mrs. Wilding, from her place a few yards away, sees the girl's face as she goes.

"I'm afraid ' Mis'Chance ' has been a little more chancy than usual this time," says she to herself. " She has evidently been resurrecting that story about Captain Stairs and Mrs. Gaveston." And forthwith goes up to the widow, who is now being severely condemned by her brother.

"You look a little upset," says Mrs. Wilding lightly.

"Who? I?" smiling with some difficulty. "Miss Prendergast looks upset, if you like, and only because I hinted——"

"No. No! I hate hearing about hints," says Mrs. Wilding, putting up her perfectly-gloved hand. "And," naïvely, "that is such a dreadfully old story, isn't it? No one with a grain of sense believes in it now. Why pick up the ashes of an agony that is quite burnt out? You know he is leaving this evening."

"Yes." Mrs. Chance's smile takes a little vicious turn. "I hope he *will go alone!*" says she.

Her brother casts an annihilating glance at her.

CHAPTER III.

"I will not let thee go,
Ends all our month-long love in this?
Can it be summed up so,
Quit in a single kiss?
I will not let thee go."

THEY are all gone now. Nell has walked up the avenue with Mr. Nobbs and Grant, the latter giving way to curses, "not loud but deep," directed against the stupid little toady, who, perhaps after all, is not so stupid, as no cause for leaving Nell and Grant alone together is apparent to him, Nell's attentions to himself being decidedly marked! She seems indeed almost to *cling* to Mr. Nobbs, and when Geoffrey, running after her, steps to her side—the side near Nobbs, she draws him over to the other side, slipping her arm round his neck, thus putting Grant even farther from her, but all in the sweetest way, and always giving her best and prettiest smiles to Grant. She is feeling almost happy, sure in the belief that Cecilia is coming on, behind her, with Mrs. Wilding.

But Cecilia had stopped at the last step of the stone staircase leading to the terrace, with Stairs beside her, and had there bidden Mrs. Wilding and her husband " good-bye."

As they turn the corner where the escalonia bush hides the terrace from view, Stairs turns to her quickly.

"Give me half-an-hour before I go. Let me bid you good-bye alone!"

Cecilia's eyes fill with tears.

"Ah! you won't go," says she. And with this grief-lorn light within her eyes, she leads the way to the eastern garden, the "Old Garden," as it is called; and indeed a sweet, old-fashioned spot it is, filled with old flowers, and older memories and griefs and joys of many a hundred years. It had belonged to the Gavestons for generations untold; it had been planned and laid out by them.

A little summer-house stands in a far corner. Having reached it—it is Cecilia's favourite resort—she turns to him.

"You don't really mean it, do you?" says she. "Of course," with a little nervous laugh. "I know you *meant* to go. But there is no such great hurry, is there?"

"I shall go," says he with determination. "Do not let us waste our last moments over an argument so vain as that."

"Why should it be vain? Peter will come back to-night, and——"

He makes an impatient movement.

"Can't you see that is why I shall go?"

"Oh, *no!* That is why you can stay." She looks mournfully at him. "I know how horrid people can be; what unpleasant things they can say. But when Peter is here——"

Stairs checks her by a gesture. Does she know what she is saying—the horrible dishonour of it? No, surely she cannot.

And indeed she does not. She is looking at him with open grief, with deepest misery. There is no undercurrent of meaning in her eyes. He will go, unless she can make him stay, and if he goes she will be wretched—that is all.

"Come, *think*, Cecilia!" says he almost

roughly. "God knows the word honour is a poor thing on my tongue, but such as it is it has some small life in it yet. Do you think I can stay beneath the roof of your husband, loving you as I do?" His voice is agitated, the remembrance of Peter, kind and hospitable, has come back to him. "I cannot! It is impossible."

"Oh, why talk of love?" says she eagerly. "We are friends?" She breaks off, and her face changes. "However!" says she, pausing, as if thinking—perhaps it is the first time thought has ever stirred her greatly in all her life. "If it is your honour," she pauses again, and bursts into tears. "Go then! I would not have you afterwards look back, and perhaps hate me."

"I shall never do anything but love you," says he with mournful conviction.

"Honour!" she repeats the word as if it is strange to her, and yet as if it touched some new untried string within her breast. "Do you know, Phil, I have sometimes thought of telling Peter . . . about it . . . our old love, I mean . . ."

"Don't," says Stairs, interrupting her, almost fiercely. "Would you destroy the only good that remains to you? I am going—he will remain. I shall in an hour drop out of your life for ever, he——"

"In an hour!" She seems to have heard only those words. "You don't mean it *really*, Phil. You won't go so *soon*. You will wait a day—a day or so—just a few little hours. See now, Phil," with a sad attempt at reasoning calmly, "what a little time it is out of all our lives. And we are only friends — good friends, no more. People "—piteously—" can be friends without other people finding fault with them, can't they now?"

He makes her no answer. What answer is there to give, save one?

"You," she creeps closer to him, "you won't go to-night anyway. You will wait till to-morrow. To-morrow after luncheon, there is a train. And——"

"I must—I must go," says he desperately.

"But why?" She looks at him with sad eyes. She would have said more perhaps, but that something in her throat chokes her. He can see that tears are not far off, and even as he looks at her, as if too miserable to withdraw his gaze, two large drops fall down her cheeks, sadly, slowly—most forlornly.

He draws his breath quickly. A devil within him that has made a resting place in his heart for many weeks, now suddenly rises triumphant. He had known it was there, and ever since his first meeting with Cecilia he had fought it valiantly, and kept it at bay. But now its hour has come. Perhaps the perpetual wrestling has weakened Stairs, has laid his armour open, and the devil who never sleeps sees his opportunity . . . The devil who never misses one. At all events the enemy has now risen, and rushing in upon him unawares, has crushed him under, and laid his hoof upon his neck.

Conquered, Stairs' soul lies within the dust.

*　　*　　*　　*　　*

In a moment he has her in his arms, her pretty head pressed tenderly against his breast.

"*Come with me!*" says he. It is a low whisper fraught and broken with passion.

For a moment she lies within his arms, as if glad—as if thankful for the rest found there. Then she stirs—sighing—and pushes him from her, not angrily, or with disdain, but (and this he cannot fail to see) reluctantly.

"You will?" whispers he eagerly.

"No—no." There is deep regret in her voice.

"Why not?" impatiently. "Are our lives given us to be made the jests of time? And what is your life here to you? And what is my life anywhere without you? My darling! My own!" He draws her to him, holding her hands only, this time however—he loves her too much not to respect her, and he remembers her late withdrawal from him. "You know how it is with me. It is not a moment's growth, Cecilia. It is the one love of all my life. I have never loved anyone but you. You know that! Does that not count with you?"

She looks at him, listening—trembling.

Her eyes are on his. They are troubled, mystified. Distressed by the childish uncertainty of them he draws her to him again. He does not attempt to kiss her; but passing his arm round her, he gently but with decision, draws her closer. Soon he tell himself—and a mad exultation uplifts him at the thought—she will be his for ever to hold, to cherish, to expend all his life upon.

"The feverish finger of love"

has laid itself upon his heart.

"My darling, speak to me," says he. "Come, Cissy, you *will!*" He strains her to him. "Decide—decide," cries he feverishly. "There is so little time!"

"Oh, don't ask me that," gasps she faintly. "Anything else—but to go—to go——" She is trembling violently, and he is still holding her. "There is Peter," says she, almost indistinctly, so low has her voice fallen. "He has trusted me. It would be better"—her voice is now anguished, "to die, than to betray his trust. And, indeed,

Phil, I would gladly die now, but death," sadly, "will not come near me."

Stairs, letting her go, turns and walks abruptly up and down.

"If he cared—if he cared, even half as much as I do."

"He *does* care," says she. She pauses with a little troubled air; the trouble of looking into things, has come upon her now for the first time. She seems even startled. Surely Peter cares. "You spoke of honour a little while ago," says she. "Peter's honour must be thought of too. It would touch him through *me*." She pauses again. "He has been very good to me," she bursts out at last as though against her will.

"I can believe it." Stairs' face is very pale as he says this—as he acknowledges the worth of the man who had gained so easily the treasure he had meant to conquer the world to win. "It is only I who have been bad to you!" He looks at her with deep and abiding grief within his eyes. "I have come into your life only to destroy it. And yet I swear to you, my beloved, that I fought against this hour. But it has been too strong for me. Must all our days be wasted? Must there be no sunshine on our paths? Will you hold back for ever—*Cissy!*"

It is a note of passion.

His arms are round her again. They hold her, and she alas! is willing to be held.

"Come with me," whispers he, his lips against her ear. "Come. It will be but a moment's trouble—and after *that*——" His voice now, though still low, rings gloriously. "After that——" He holds her back from him, her sudden surrender has made him madly happy. His face is white, but his eyes are lit with a glad, wild light. "After that we shall be always together — *together* — always! My darling! My life, have you thought of it? Do you know half of what you are to me, how I idolize—how I adore you?"

"Oh!" murmurs she softly. The half articulate sound seems to come from her heart; she clings to him. Her cheek is lying against his. He has won then! His clasp tightens round her.

CHAPTER IV.

"Nay, if they will not turn, there is blackness of darkness
  before them,
Lurid with lights that lead only to uttermost hell."

NELL, in the morning-room, with little Geoffrey on his knees in one of the windows, building houses out of cards, is walking, with momentarily increasing restlessness, from the window to her chair, and back again. When will Cecilia come in? How long—how *long* has she been out there—in the garden.

Impatiently, and in a half-frightened way, she presses her hands together, staring through the window into the fast-gathering dusk outside. It is now six o'clock, and Philip's train goes at seven. She is aware that she has told herself this, half-a-dozen times during the last hour—the repetition of it being due to the fact that she is dwelling with thankfulness on the thought that soon he will be outside Cecilia's life—at all events for awhile, and, with any luck, for ever. But why doesn't Cecilia come in? Surely she has not been mad enough to try and persuade him to prolong his stay. And yet —it would be so like Cecilia!

Again another rapid walk to the window that overlooks the garden path!

What *can* be keeping her? There is but little time left now, if he really means to catch his train, as the drive to the station will take at least fifteen minutes, and there are always little last things to be done and said; the bringing down of the portmanteaus, the good-byes, the sudden memories of the most important matters of all, left to the last, and nearly forgotten — the book for the journey, left on the toilet table so as to make quite sure of its being remembered.

And the train goes at seven—and Philip with it, thank goodness! Why doesn't he come in? Every moment is growing precious. Her eyes are staring again along the garden path, but no moving thing meets her view. Shall she send a servant to warn him of the passing hour? That seems so cold, so unfriendly. And his journey will be a very lonely one, poor fellow——

Suddenly, from nowhere, as it were, a frightful fear springs to life within her breast. A hot burning colour dyes her cheeks, then fades away, leaving her ghastly. A sensation of faintness renders her cold, lifeless. Was it that word " lonely " that suggested the terrible thing?

That cruel rush of cold to her heart has gone now, and once again she stares eagerly into the calm of the gathering night. Where—where is Cecilia? Dear Heaven! why isn't Peter at home? Is there *no* one to help her? No one!

The fear grows stronger — surer. Her thoughts are hardly to be endured. Clutching a fold of the amber curtain as if to steady herself, she combats them with all her might, but still they grow—looming large through the soft mist of the coming night outside. She becomes conscious presently that she is trembling in every limb. The train—Philip will go by it, but not alone. . . . *Cecilia will go too!*

It seems quite an old, old thought now, in the dull certainty of it. She turns to the door mechanically, telling herself she must go to her, but pauses suddenly near the round oak table. Even if she did go, of what use would she be?—with no authority behind her, with Peter so many miles away. If a woman could give up husband and position and reputation so easily, how much more easily a sister!

Still to go! She ought—she must. The ordeal seems more than the poor child can bring herself to endure, but there is a good deal of strength underlying the frivolity of her nature that, perhaps, only wants occasion to bring it to the front. She *will* go to her, and hold her back, with all the strength of her young, strong arms, if it comes to that. And she could so hold her; Cecilia, so slender, so delicate, would be no match for her. She takes another step towards the door, and then again she stops. Is Cecilia there to hold? Is she already gone?

She leans against the table; her hand, pressing upon it, keeps her steady. Again that dreadful faintness sweeps over her, and through it comes the sound of the boy's playing with the cards in the distant corner. There is a little dull "*fll*," that tells of the cards' collapse. Once again the Chinese pagoda has been laid low!

Geoffrey gives way to a groan of disgust—*four* storeys high, and now a ruin! Never mind, ruins can be rebuilt with energetic little hands, and the indomitable courage of youth. He gathers together the cards again, and begins a fresh castle.

Nell, roused by the sound of the boy's play, has turned her frightened eyes upon him. Why, here—here is the finest help of all—if only help has not arrived too late. The blood springs into her cheek, and courage once more fills her bosom. The child! Her *child*.

"Geoffrey," calls she eagerly.

"Yes," returns the boy slowly, absently. Already the fresh pagoda is a storey high, and the interest in it is absorbing.

"Come here, darling. Come quickly. Oh, *come*, Geoffrey."

"In a minute," says Geoffrey, kindly and courteously, but how could one expect one to "come quickly" when one is building houses out of cards? And already his erection has gained a second storey. He is building rapidly, and with success—the second storey stands firm and strong.

"Don't mind that, Geoff! Come here," says Nell, so fiercely, and with such a stamp of her little foot, that the boy, astonished, looks up at her, a card in his hand (the first brick for the third storey), and surprise in his sunny eyes.

"Geoffrey," says Nell, dropping on her knees beside him, "will you do something for me?"

The child looks at her, still clutching the card, however.

"I will," says he at last, after considerable hesitation, and two backward glances at the rising palace behind him.

"Oh, I knew you would," says his auntie, catching him in her arms, and smothering him with kisses, a process against which he most actively rebels. "You will run down

to the garden, won't you? Now this minute.
To your mother—to the little summer house
—the little summer house she loves so much,
and tell her—tell her——"

Here a sudden storm of grief overcomes
her, choking her voice, and making her eyes
blind with tears. Oh! to have to ask the
boy to save his mother—and yet, what surer
messenger? Whose charm so strong as his?
It is a last—her only resource as it seems to
Nell, whose strange, unaccountable fear is
killing her.

"To go to mammy?" questions the child
vaguely.

"Yes. Yes, my darling." Nell is sobbing
uncontrollably now, though silently—holding
the boy to her to conceal from him her grief.
"Go there, and look for mammy, and if she is
not there, go to the upper garden, that overlooks the sea—she loves that place too, and
tell her——"

"What'll I tell her?"

"Oh, nothing—nothing!" Nell has risen
to her feet, she has choked back her tears,
and is standing pale and shaken before the

child. "Just run to her, with your arms out like this"—holding out her own arms eagerly—" and fling them round her neck like *this*," catching the boy to her, and holding him against her heart.

"Yes—but——" The child, not understanding, hesitates, casting fond glances backwards at his growing palace. How firm it stands. It will not fall *this* time!

"Never mind your house. I'll take care of it till you come back," says Nell feverishly. Alas! in what a house of cards his mother now is dwelling! "Go now, Geoff, darling ——go—and *hurry!*"

"But why?" asks the child reluctantly, who naturally cannot see why he is required to go and hug his mother, on this particular occasion; she can always be hugged as often as ever she likes—and to go now, when his house is in danger. He casts another longing glance back at it—the two storeys still stand grandly firm.

"Because I ask you. Isn't Nellie—" with a wheedling voice that is stricken with misery, "your own old auntie? Won't you do something for her? You *will* go to your mammy, won't you, ducky? Oh, you will, Geoffrey"—passionately. "And you will throw your arms round her and kiss her—and kiss her"—in spite of her, her tears break out again here—" your *own* mammy, Geoffrey. Your own mammy, remember. She wants you, darling, she does indeed."

"Did she send for me?" asks the boy.

"Yes." Nell tells her lie without a qualm.

"But she'll be coming in now, won't she? And I"—with considerable pride, "want to show her my house when it's done. It'll be a big one this time, there'll be *four* of them if nobody shakes it."

It seems hopeless! Even her own child won't help her. Nell almost thrusts him from her, and then another chance occurs to her. She makes a last move.

"It is time for you to go to bed," says she coldly. "You surely will not go without bidding your mammy good-night."

"It isn't time yet," says the child startled.

"Yes—it is."

"But mammy——"

"She is out in the garden. Go and bid her good-night—and go quickly." The child rises and moves towards the window that opens on to the verandah.

"She'll let me finish it," says he.

"Yes," says Nell eagerly. She almost pushes the child onwards. "And remember what I told you. Your mammy is not happy. Geoff—*make* her happy! Throw your arms round her, and kiss her, and hold her, and *keep* her! Oh, Geoffrey!"

Nell's voice dies away; the boy has fled down the steps and into the gathering darkness, and now she is at peace to cry her eyes out. If the child should fail. . . . If she should be already gone. . . .

Oh, the relief of being alone! She sinks into a chair—covering her face with her hands—and sobs as if her heart would break, for a minute or two. Then she pulls herself together with the strength—the perpetual springing of hope—that belongs to youth only. It is what we moderns call a revulsion of feeling. Why, how foolish she has been. Of course it was impossible; she must have been mad to think such thoughts of Cissy. Why, if she knew, she would never forgive her . . . . But she should never know. Poor Cissy—dear Cissy! . . . Was there ever a wrong thought in her mind? Oh, she trusted her—completely—perfectly!

But the child! How *long* he is! Will he never come back—will she *never* know!

CHAPTER V.

> "Oh thou bright thing, fresh from the hand of God!"
> * * * * * *
> "Look how he laughs and stretches out his arms,
> And opens wide his blue eyes upon thine."

It is the eleventh hour indeed! Cecilia with her lover's arms around her has yielded. Yes—she will go with him. She has only to throw on her hat, her coat——a short walk through the woods will bring her to the station in ten minutes. She——

"Mammy! Mammy! Where are you?"

The high, sweet cry of a child—the patter of little sturdy feet upon the gravelled path —the sight of a little handsome boy racing with all his might—capless, and with his bonny tight-cropped head thrown back.

Cecilia almost *thrusts* Stairs from her. An awful look comes into her eyes.

"My God! I had forgotten him!" says she.

She shrinks backwards, almost cowering

before the child who, now having seen her, casts himself with a little merry cry into her arms. The arms that for the first time in all his adored little life, feel slack, loveless. It is not the want of love that makes them weak—fear and shame, and passionate self-reproach render Cecilia cold.

"Nellie told me I'd find you here," says the boy gaily. "You're to come in, she says, and I was to kiss you like this, and like this." He has pulled down his young mother's head to his, with his fond, stout, little arms, and is kissing her, with a laugh between every kiss. "You must come in at once, because it's nearly time for me to go to bed, and I want to finish my house first."

"I'll come—in a minute, Geoffrey," says his mother in a choking voice.

"No, now—now!" with childish persistency, "I want to say my prayers to you."

Another stab.

"Last time I didn't say my prayers to you I was very ill after it. 'Member?"

It was a year ago, and something had prevented her hearing the child say his simple prayers. "Our Father" first, and then "God bless Pappy and Mammy"; and it so happened that next day he developed a cold and was confined to his bed for some days. With a child's queer reasoning he had always said that the reason he was ill was because he had not said his prayers at his mother's knee.

Ill. If he should be really ill, when she was miles and miles away from him . . . separated from him by still greater barriers than time or distance—barriers of her own erection. Ill! The word rings in her ears. Dying perhaps! Perhaps *dead*—and buried, and she not even knowing.

With a frantic fervour she clasps him to her breast—holding him convulsively to her; slowly she turns her eyes on Stairs.

"Go!" says she, framing the word with difficulty.

"You have decided?" His voice is cold and strange. He had known, from the moment of the boy's coming, how it would be. The terrible look in her eyes was not to be mistaken. The child had dashed aside his chance for ever. He had come five minutes too soon. She *had* given up her husband—she would *not* give up the child.

"You must see," whispers she in a voice of anguish, pressing the little one's head against her bosom, as though to prevent his hearing.

"Perfectly! You had to choose between —him—and me, and you have chosen the child. *His* child!"

"No—mine—*mine!* My own——" She pauses as if spent. "He is my soul! Shall I destroy him? When he grew up—to hear of me—to think with scorn of me . . how would it be then? *Now* he loves me! . . . *Then!* . . ."

"It is all over then?" says he brusquely.

"I cannot!"

"It is the last word, Cecilia?"

"Yes," in a dying tone.

The child, struggling in her embrace, has now freed himself, and is looking anxiously from his mother to Stairs.

"You are crying," says he, peering at his mother in the now uncertain light—then turning upon Stairs, whom, with all a child's curious instinct, he had never liked, he breaks out, "I hate you! It is you—it is *you* who are making her cry."

"Oh! Geoffrey, no; not a word, my darling!"

Again she presses his head against her, as though to hide from him her face, and looks with anguished eyes upon her lover. Dumbly she holds out to him her hand. He takes it mechanically, then drops it and turns to go.

At this, a low but bitter cry escapes her.

"Phil, Phil!" She sways a little towards him, holding out to him again, the hand he has so coldly dropped, whilst keeping the other still clasped around the boy. "A moment—you will not go—like this—you"— gasping—"will bid me good-bye?"

For a while they so stand staring into each other's eyes—she so white in her misery—he with a face full of the bitterness of death. Then he steps deliberately out of the summer-house, and disappears into the night mist beyond.

*　　*　　*　　*　　*

Silence has fallen on the garden.

The rejected hand has slowly joined the other, and is now clasped around the child's neck. Cecilia has sunk into a chair and Geoffrey, uncertain, but a little frightened, has crept into her lap.

Outside, a sudden, gentle rising of the wind, has shaken a leaf or two from the rose-bush near, and far away beyond the hills over there, a young bright moon is standing, within a dazzling field of purple, shading to darkest grey.

"Mammy," says the child nervously, "why don't you come in? Are you crying again?"

"No, no."

"Your hands are very cold! I want to go in. I——" whimpering, "I'm cold, too. I'm tired. I'm sleepy!"

"Wait a while—a little while, my darling, with your Mammy—your poor Mammy."

He must be going now. In another minute or so he will be gone. Her heart is dying within her—her knees feel weak; the effort to rise, to stir is beyond her. Now—what was that? The sound of carriage wheels? Now he is gone! gone—for ever! She has sent him from her——

"Phil——"

She starts to her feet with a stifled cry, still holding the child, but gazing before her, listening always to the departing wheels, her eyes straining into the night.

"What is it, Mammy?" whispers the child, his voice beginning to quiver. Presently he bursts out crying.

"Don't, don't! My darling, my delight. Don't cry. It is nothing—nothing at all, my sweetheart. There, come, we will go in! And he will love his poor Mammy always, and he will always remember that she loved him beyond all, beyond everything—beyond life itself!"

CHAPTER VI.

"Even ev'ry ray of hope destroyed,
And not a *wish* to gild the gloom."

CECILIA has pushed back the curtains that hide the window leading on to the verandah, and has stumbled into the room before Nell sees her.

"Oh! Thank God!" cries the girl fervently, forgetting herself in the strain of the moment. How is she to explain her thankfulness further on? "Oh! Cissy. You have come. . . . . You——"

She stops short abruptly. Cecilia's face is ghastly! Is it Cecilia at all? *This* woman is ten years older than the Cecilia of the afternoon. The change in her terrifies Nell. She runs to her and would have caught her, but Cecilia thrusts her back—even in this supreme moment, the action is singularly graceful.

"Let me alone!" says she. Her soft, sweet

voice is hardly recognisable. She has moved forward, but now she looks back at Nell. "He is *gone!*"

The words break from her in a little burst, as though it were impossible to keep them back. Nell, who is like a sheet of paper herself, sends up silently a fervent thanksgiving to Heaven.

"Gone?"

"Yes—for ever," says Cecilia stupidly as if dazed. Then all at once her manner changes. Life comes into her face again. "Oh, no; he can't be gone yet," cries she. She hurries towards the window, and drags the curtains aside in a frenzied fashion. "There may yet be time . . ."

She has forgotten the sound of those wheels now lost and gone.

"Are you *mad?*" says Nell sternly, going quickly forward, and getting between her and the window; "you *shall* not go! You shall stay here! Cecilia, are you lost to all sense of honour? He is gone—gone, Cissy! And I thank God for his going!"

"Oh Nell! Oh, Nell!" says Cecilia. Her

voice eats into Nell's heart. She does not resist in any way. Indeed, she lets Nell lead her back and press her into a chair, where she lies as if exhausted. She has clasped her hands over her eyes.

"How shall I bear it? How?" A convulsive shudder shakes her slender body. Suddenly she springs up. "I can't bear it! I won't! Nell, have pity! You are the only one who can help me! Help me now! I *must* see him again—some way—and soon— soon. If I wrote to him. . ."

She breaks into wild weeping.

"Hush!" says Nell, almost violently. "Do you want the servants to hear?"

She catches Cecilia, and folding her arms about her, presses her to her, so that her sobs may not be heard. She herself, poor child, is shaking all over, yet still a great courage is with her . . . And God be thanked, Peter is away.

"Come upstairs," says she in a low tone, but with authority.

At any moment a servant may come in, and servants, given one glance, know *every-*

thing. Servants are the cleverest class in the world.

She slips her hand through Cecilia's arm, and Cecilia, when her sobs have grown fewer, allows her to guide her from the room and upstairs, a little journey accomplished by Nell in fear and trembling. But providentially all the women-servants are downstairs at this time, and she gets Cecilia into her room without encountering anyone.

"We shall be quiet here. You told Marshall you would not dress to-night, did you not? Lie back there, and rest, and do not talk."

"I must talk to you," says Cecilia. "I must tell you, Nell—you will listen? Oh, the comfort of *saying* it all."

"Don't say too much," says Nell a trifle grimly. "There is always to-morrow!"

"To-morrow!" Cecilia looks at her, as if only half understanding; then the misery in her eyes grows if possible deeper. "Oh, dear Heaven! it is true!" cries she. "To-morrow —and the to-morrow after that—and days and years—*years*, Nell! How am I to live them out? Oh! why did I let him go? He wanted me to go with him, and I refused—*refused.*"

"Don't talk like that," says the girl. "Don't!—I tell you, you will be sorry; you have a husband and——"

"I know it"—passionately. "Does one forget one's chief misfortune? I have a husband who was forced upon me when I was a mere child—when I did not know what I was doing; when I was a girl younger than you are now. I knew nothing then, but I know *now* what I did, I threw away my life, my soul, my happiness! What is Peter to me? I tell you"—she rises suddenly and flings out her arms with a tragic gesture—"I would gladly see him *dead* rather than that Philip should endure one pang."

"You don't know what you are saying," says Nell. She is terribly agitated. "To speak of Peter like that. Peter, who loves you, who trusts you!" Cecilia makes a terrible movement. "Oh, darling, darling, think." All at once her grief overpowers her, and she gives way. Sinking at Cecilia's feet, she clasps her arms round her. "I know—I *know* that you are suffering, but think of Peter, Cissy, think of the man who——"

"I can't," says Cecilia stonily. She makes a faint effort to push the girl from her, but Nell still clings to her, crying bitterly but noiselessly, her face hidden against her sister's skirts. "I can think of nothing but my lost youth — my lost happiness — my dead life. All is over. All. I tell you, Nell, I have not one thought left for Peter. I was sold to him——"

"But he did not know."

"Nevertheless he must take the consequences. He"—with a cruel judging, that seems to transform her — "should have known."

"Still—he didn't," pleads Nell. "And he has loved you—been good to you. He is your husband. Cecilia, you *must* remember you have a husband and a——"

"No. No." Cecilia breaks from her embrace, and Nell rises slowly to her feet.

The face of the child is before them both.
"I forbid you to speak of *him*."

There is a long silence, from which Cecilia is the first to recover. Her manner is a little changed now, calmer, colder.

"I know all that you would say. I am a married woman—the rights of marriage are sacred. I do not respect them, and I do not love the man to whom the law has bound me. I am therefore"—with a contemptuous laugh—"a wicked woman!"

"No. No, darling."

"You are right." She throws back her lovely head with a defiant gesture. "People may call me so, but I don't *feel* wicked. It is the world that has been wicked to me. Why should I be deprived of love and joy—*you* talk to me—you who have your life before you—who can choose this man or that for your husband—you, who have no mother to coerce you— to *lie* to you—to——" She breaks off suddenly, and begins to pace, with quick, uneven steps, up and down the room.

"It was hard," says Nell, in a low tone, broken, sweet, sympathetic. It touches the wounded heart. Cecilia, stopping short, looks at her.

"Hard! That is the word. You feel for me then? You understand—you do not condemn!"

"Oh! Cissy! You *know* I don't."

* * * * *

"Dinner will be ready in half an hour," says Nell presently—a fresh anxiety springing to life. "You must bathe your eyes."

"I can't go downstairs," says Cecilia. "Nellie—arrange it."

"We can have a tray sent up here then."

Sometimes when Peter had gone on magisterial business to one of the county towns, the sisters had preferred a little unceremonious meal to be sent up to them to Cecilia's dainty boudoir, to the more prolonged dinner downstairs in the big dining-room.

"It will be all right—I'll speak to James presently. Now *do* try and take a little rest."

"Yes—yes." She leans back, sighing, heavily, but almost immediately looks up again. "Did he—did he say good-bye to you?"

"No," stoutly. "I suppose he had *some* sense of decency left. He must have understood why I sent——"

She stops. She had not meant to betray her part in the affair, but it is too late now to retract.

"*You* sent Geoffrey to the garden?"

"Yes," says Nell, disdaining to compromise. "I sent him, and whatever *you* may think of it—I shall always regard it as the best action of my life. You ought to be very grateful to me."

"Ought I?" says poor Cecilia. She turns away, and the tears run down her cheeks afresh. "I suppose so. But"—plaintively —"*I'm not.*"

"Look here," says Nell presently, when she has bathed her forehead with eau de Cologne, and restored her to calm again. "Peter will be back again at half-past eleven at latest, and you will have to see *him.*"

"I will not," says Cecilia, with sudden, strange determination.

"But——"

"I *will* not! Tell him I have a headache.

Tell him anything you like. I shall certainly not see him."

"But is this wise, Cissy? Surely he will think—connect——"

"I don't care what he thinks," says Cecilia doggedly, and, indeed, this proves final. Nell, after five minutes' further argument, finds it impossible to move her.

Dinner comes, and, the sorry pretence at eating it being at an end, Cecilia decides on going to bed.

"I'm tired. I'm worn out, Nellie."

"I know. I'll put you to bed. *Poor* old ducky!"

Tenderly—with the most loving care Nell undresses her, and brushes her hair, and finally tucks her into her bed.

"Good night now, darling, and try to sleep."

"I will—I will, indeed," says Cecilia obediently, who feels as though she will never go to sleep again. And Nell, turning away, she puts out a hand and catches her. To be left alone. . . .

"Nell—a moment. . . ."

"Yes, darling. Would you like me to stay with you?"

"Oh! I *should*. But—you are tired."

"I am not, indeed."

"Yes, you are! I know you are. But, Nellie"—she draws up the sheet over her face, as if to hide it, in a childish way—"he said something to me about—about *honour!*"

"Oh, *his* honour!" says Nell contemptuously, but so low that Cecilia does not hear her.

"Yes! Honour! Well, I have saved his honour, Nell. But—*I have broken my own heart!*"

"Cissy!"

Nell tries to pull down the sheet, and look at her, but she resists strongly.

"Oh, Cissy darling, what can I do for you?"

"What can anyone do for me?"

There is a pause, and presently, in a stifled voice, she says:

"Bring Geoff to me."

Nell, running into the nursery, lifts the boy —so rosy and so sweet in his happy dreaming, and gives him, only half awake, into his mother's arms.

"Mammy," says he drowsily, but so happily. It is one of his many treats to sleep with his "Mammy." Nell sees Cecilia's arms close round him, sees her eager kiss upon his pretty cheek, sees the almost convulsive clutching to her of the loved little form—and lowering the lamp, she steps lightly from the room. If anything can cure this cruel wound, surely the child's arms will!

* * * * *

Half-past eleven has struck, and Nell, stepping out into the corridor, meets Gaveston as he comes up the stairs. She lays her fingers on her lips. Cecilia has had one of her headaches, she explains to him. She, Nell, had taken Geoffrey to sleep with her. Both are asleep now. He must be careful not to disturb them.

Of course he will be careful. On tiptoe he creeps to his wife's room, and having laid the candlestick on the floor, leans over her and his child.

Such a lovely pair! The faces so alike—

and one scarcely younger than the other. The child's arms are flung wide, in all the happy abandonment of childhood, but the mother's arms are fondly clasped around the little shapely body.

But how pale Cecilia looks. What circles lie beneath her eyes. Her headache has been bad, poor darling! Nell had not made enough of it! But no doubt this sound sleep will chase it all away!

Noiselessly he withdraws from the room, and as the door closes behind him, Cecilia stirs. Softly bringing one of the sleeping child's hands to her lips, she presses kiss upon kiss on it—then breaks into bitter tears.

CHAPTER VII.

"When a man is old,
And the weather blowes cold,
   Well fare a fire and a furred gowne;
But when he is young,
And his blood new sprung,
   His sweetheart is wirth halfe the towne!"

IT is a month later, and Nell, filled with joy at the beauty of this sweet September day, has decided on going for one of her long, lonely rides across the downs. No groom for her on these wild, happy excursions, only her pretty bay mare—"Miss Jenkins," to keep her company.

Down through the woodland path, where the beech-leaves are making a copper carpet for her horse's feet, and out into the open ground beyond—up the big hill, and so on to the high level sweep of country, from which one can see the ocean for miles and miles. The smell of the sea-weed is in the air to-day, and the heavy gorgeous purple of the

heather is decorating the whole wide world—
so far as she can see. There is a splendid
majesty about the sombre glory of this
autumn day.

"September, all glorious with gold as a king,
  In radiance attired,
Outlightening the summer, outsweetening the spring,
Broods wide on the woodlands with limitless wing,
  A presence of all men desired."

Oh! how sweet it is up here with the salt spray casting its fragrance towards her, and the sun glistening and playing with the waves, that seem so many *years* away down here. She pulls rein, and letting Miss Jenkins fret a little, gazes thoughtfully at the sea. That great thing! How free it is, tossing this way and that at its own free will—so calm, so solemn, so entirely without care! If you had told her at this moment that there were such rude tyrants as tides to hold this seemingly-free ocean in check, and that there was even a moon to check the tides, it might perhaps have taken something from her admiration of the ocean's freedom, and certainly you would have displeased her. Presently Miss Jenkins, having protested overmuch at the enforced delay, Nell continues her way across the downs, the mare breaking unforbidden into a light canter. It seems to set itself to music, and presently Nell finds herself singing:

> "Oh! who will o'er the downs with me?
> Oh! who will with me ride?
> Oh! who will up and follow me,
> To win a blooming bride?"

Suddenly she bursts out laughing. Perhaps it is the ozone that has got into her head, but certainly she has not felt so joyous for weeks as she does to-day. What a ridiculous glee! Were they all . . . *all* the followers to win "the blooming bride?" And "blooming"—how the word has lost its first fresh meaning? It sounds now like a costermonger's ditty addressed to his young woman. But costermongers, as a rule, don't run away with their young ladies on horseback—they content themselves with a wedding trip on "A Bicycle made for Two," if one can depend on those who attempt to explain their manners and little eccentricities.

Miss Jenkins has now taken a small fence

that stood in her way—a way that leads into the woods of "Strange," and the thread of Nell's thoughts is broken.

> "My father, he has locked the door,
> My mother keeps the key.
> But neither locks nor bars can keep
> My own true love from me!"

What a terribly determined person! Thank goodness people are not so determined now-a-days. But even if they were; well—there's one thing, she will not be anyone's "blooming bride" for many a year yet—if at all. No! marriage is a mistake. Poor Cissy's failure is always before her. An ever freshly recurring grief.

She is in the "Strange" wood now, and even as her thoughts take this heroic turn, she finds herself looking at Grant, who is riding towards her through the trees, evidently in mad haste.

Now, part of her desire to enjoy this exquisite day alone, had arisen out of a determination to avoid "the coming man." She had seen him yesterday, and he had expressed a determination to come over and see Cecilia to-day. One could easily know what *that* meant. Cecilia would give him tea, an hour after he arrived, and Cecilia would disappear for another hour after that; and this troublesome Captain Grant had been pressing his suit with her—Nell—somewhat vigorously during the past fortnight.

How idiotically Time (old as he is, he might surely know *something!*) arranges matters. Why on earth should Alec be here, of all places, at this hour? The sun and the earth refuse to answer this leading question, and there he is certainly, at all events.

" How d'ye do ? " says she ever so pleasantly, and trying to keep a guilty look out of her eyes. It is impossible to put out of sight the fact that he had told her that he would be at The Park at five, and here is she, at half-past four, riding leisurely in the opposite direction. He had told her too, that he would have to spend his morning at the McGregors', who were getting up private theatricals, so that he could hardly lay the flattering unction to his soul, that she had come this way to meet him, as the McGregors live in exactly the opposite direction.

"Quite well, thank you," returns he ironically, dropping to the ground, and going up to her, his horse's bridle over his arm. "I needn't ask how you are—this long ride from your home assures me of your health. Are you coming back to tea?"

"Did you expect me to be there? You told me you were going to see Cecilia."

"Nell! Is that honest?"

"I don't see why I am to be accused of dishonesty," says the girl, flushing in spite of herself, and playing somewhat nervously with her reins.

"Don't you? You knew very well," says the young man, breaking into open wrath, "that I was going over to The Park to-day to see you. Will you deny *that?*"

"Have I denied anything? Even," her own anger rising now, "if I did know you were going, why should I be accused of—of very unpleasant things, because I choose to go for a ride instead of staying in for afternoon-tea? Supposing I had a headache and wished to ride it off? . . ."

"Had you a headache?" His manner has now all the determination of one who means to elicit an answer, whether she wishes to give it or not. It is a sort of bringing her to bay that annoys Nell.

"No; I had not," says she slowly, and with distinct defiance.

"That is not to be misunderstood at all events," says he coldly. He turns away, but even with his foot in the stirrup—he hesitates, and as a consequence is lost.

In a moment he is at her side again.

"Nell—it is useless. I can't go—not while there is the smallest chance of getting you. And as long as you don't love any other fellow, there may be that."

He pauses, as if waiting for a denial from her as to the other possible chance. The denial does not come.

"You don't?"

"No—no. Of course not," hastily. "I" —impatiently—" am quite *tired* of telling you that."

"I'm not tired of hearing it."

Miss Prendergast makes a little angry movement, and turning in her saddle looks through the trees to where a glimpse of the ocean can still be seen. The horses have lowered their heads, and are nibbling with a rather dignified air, the long unsavoury grass that grows beneath trees.

"Don't turn from me like that, Nell. Is it because I tell you that you are the only woman in the world I want to marry, that you should treat me with disdain?"

"I don't treat you with disdain. I treat you just as I do anyone else. But—why can't you see it? I don't want to be married *at all!*" She has not turned her head towards him, she is still gazing out at the glimpse of the ocean, that shows between the trees, so free, so calm. She too wants to be free. . . To go her own way, to have no control over her, no one to ask why she travels this path, or that. Cecilia's marriage is ever before her. What a terrible mistake that had been—and is any marriage very happy?

"You know you don't mean that," says he.

"I do. I want to be an old maid."

"Nonsense."

Perhaps looking at her, there is some justification for this rude remark.

"I want to be free anyway," says she slowly.

"But in a year or two. Perhaps then you would listen to me. Perhaps then you would tire of freedom."

"Never. Never."

"How can you tell? A year makes a great difference. Give me *some* hope, Nell."

"What can I say to convince you?" cries she in despair. "Surely this is hard on me. What hope *is* there to give?"

"It is true, however, what you said just now—that there is no hope for any other man."

"How persistent you are," faintly smiling. "No! there is no hope for any other man or," laughing, "you either. Not——" She holds out her hand to him kindly, and in the thankful spirit of one who has found a way of escape out of her trouble, "not a *scrap*."

"I may believe you?" taking the hand and holding it as though it were a relic.

"You may," eagerly, "you may indeed." She is bending slightly from her saddle, and Grant is looking up at her with undeniable devotion in his gaze. It is perhaps a little unfortunate that Wortley should have chosen this moment of all others—gun in hand—to step on to the top of a wall that leads into a field some distance away. From there he has a clear view of the two below—of Nell bending towards Grant—of Grant holding her hand. Of the two faces, so close together—so earnest!

CHAPTER VIII.

"The whimpering winds have lost their way;
    Weep, yaffel, weep from tree to tree;
The trunks stand grim and the fields stretch gray,
And, the year that is dead, is dead for aye:
    Weep, yaffel, weep from tree to tree."

WITH a sharp ejaculation he drops from the wall back into the field from which he has just come. To look further is impossible, though he would have given half he is worth to see; but it is with a sense of passionate disgust that he leans against the wall, and lets his mind dwell on the picture he has just seen. What a *contemptible* flirt! And without a particle of principle! She had lied to him freely about Grant—he has seen enough with his own eyes now, to convince him for ever of that, and no doubt she had not been quite truthful about her relations with Stairs.

There had been some foolish gossip in the neighbourhood about Stairs and her sister, Mrs. Gaveston, but people, as some wise person has discovered, are "mostly fools," and

Miss Prendergast had undoubtedly befooled them to the top of her bent. It seems even possible that this accomplished coquette had used her own sister as a blind to hide her flirtations.

At all events she has befooled him twice. He had believed her when she told him Grant was nothing to her—twice he had believed that, and now with this evidence——

There is an old proverb, that "the third is the charm." *Her* third time has come, and the charm is—with him now, he has seen—he knows.

The soft trample of horses' hoofs across the field behind him sharpens his thoughts. In another moment Miss Prendergast's mare has cleared a small break in the wall, and is advancing towards him.

"You, Sir Stephen? You have been killing some poor pretty thing of course?"

She makes a gesture towards the gun on his shoulder, and her manner is meant to be, as usual, as indifferent as possible. But it is clear all the same that his appearance has disturbed her in an extraordinary degree. To him, it occurs that she is afraid of his having seen her just now with Grant. To her——

"No. I have been very unfortunate so far. If I had said that to you, it might have had more meaning."

"You think *I* have been killing something then? But Miss Jenkins, as you see, is quite fresh."

"She has had a long rest." To hide from her the fact that he had seen her with Grant is distasteful to his sharp sense of honour. "I saw you talking to Grant just now," he says bluntly.

"You saw?"

"Certainly I did. I couldn't help it. You might have seen me too, for the matter of that. I stood on the wall there. The world is free to everyone, you know, and I couldn't possibly have known that you were keeping a tryst with someone at the other side of it." He points to the wall.

"A tryst. Still—you say you saw—and then—— ?"

"And then I jumped down. I felt I shouldn't have seen—even so much."

"Did you? What a delicate conscience! And what was there to be seen?"

"Need I tell you?" His tone is quite as sarcastic as hers. "A very charming picture, I assure you, and highly romantic. A girl on horseback, a man, very literally at her knees. Evidently the chosen lover, as the girl's hand was tenderly clasped in his. I am sorry," says Wortley, breaking off suddenly, "that I cannot add a few more touches to the pretty scene, but as I have already told you, at that interesting stage of the proceedings, I found I ought not to be there at all, so I jumped off the wall."

"You are very clever," says Nell, her face extremely pale. "You are also," slowly, "very impertinent!"

"You wrong me there, I think," says Wortley, still with his mocking smile. "You must remember that you insisted on my telling you what I saw. Was the description not graphic enough, or too highly coloured? Where am I in fault? For my own part I see but one error in my conduct. As your guardian I should perhaps *not* have dropped off that wall—I should have kept my eye on you. But as you see, I fell short there."

"As I have just hinted, you are wonderfully conscientious."

"Am I? In a little time, to which I am sure you look forward with hope, you will be released from my conscientious care. In the meantime, it is my bounden duty to look after you—to tell you what I think of you."

" Of me ? "

" Of you."

"Then tell me!" Nell is looking at him with an air that would have daunted most men, with the contemptuous open air of a young girl who thinks she knows all things, and who in effect knows so very little. Her manner is very defiant and it is quite plain to him that she is extremely angry.

" Shall I ? "

"I hope you quite understand that you *must*," says the girl with a certain hauteur.

"'Your blood be on your own head,'" says Wortley, regarding her with exasperating calmness, "though perhaps, what I am going to say, will raise you a peg or two in your own estimation. As a fact I think you the greatest coquette it has ever been my great good fortune to meet. There! That's praise, isn't it? It is always a matter for rejoicing to be the biggest person in one's own line."

"And on what have you founded this remarkable theory of yours?" Miss Prendergast's voice sounds stifled.

"You insist on going further then." He shrugs his shoulders. "Why, there is first one lover, and then another."

He stops, and she colours hotly. Who does he mean by the other? Surely not . . . *He*—Sir Stephen—has never . . .

"I don't understand you," says she icily.

"Then you shall! First Grant, and then Stairs."

Nell draws a quick breath.

"Captain Stairs!" Her astonishment is too great for words. "You are mad"—are the words on her lips, but by a supreme effort she subdues them. Her thoughts have flown to Cecilia again. If this cannot help her. . . . All at once she determines to accept the situation for Cecilia's sake.

"Yes—Stairs." He looks at her, expecting, hoping for a denial, but none comes.

"You don't deny it then?"

"No," haughtily, "I deny nothing."

"You have changed your tactics. Last time you denied everything."

"I am sorry I went to so much trouble. I forgot myself greatly when I did."

"You admit then that you spoke falsely to me with regard to Grant."

"I admit as little as I deny," says she, lifting her eyes suddenly to his. There is a touch of fire in them. "Has it occurred to you that you are calling me a liar?"

"No," says Wortley, whose face is now rigid. "The only thing that has occurred to me is, that you ought to be ashamed."

"So I am," she laughs suddenly, bitterly—it is the shortest, the most miserable little laugh—"*of you!*"

"It is kind of you to give me even so much attention, especially as I cannot see how it is deserved."

"Don't you? Is there nothing shameful in attacking me as you have done—of accusing me of all sorts of terrible things—of being abominably rude to me—of——"

"All this simply means," says he coldly, interrupting her without apology, "that you refuse to see yourself in the wrong."

"Wrong! There is *no* wrong."

"Of course not," with a disagreeable smile that enrages her, "women are never wrong. Let it rest there."

"No," quickly, passionately. "It shall not rest there. You *shall* speak."

"You order me about a good deal," says he in an amused sort of way that is almost cruel—"should one order one's guardian like that? You have courage for so much, but after all you have not the courage to acknowledge your own faults; to see——"

She checks him.

"Oh, courage," says she contemptuously. "The want of that is not my besetting sin. Why," leaning towards him, "as you see, I have courage enough to defy you. You," with a strange laugh, "the arbiter of my fortune, the director of my life! I defy you, for example, to tell me how I am in the wrong."

"There is no occasion for defiance," says Wortley icily. "I know you are in the wrong when — amongst *others*" — (this is bitter) " you encourage Grant without definite designs—without having made up your mind to marry him."

"Are you so sure of my mind?"

A pang that he cannot, or will not, acknowledge shoots through his heart. The girl sitting on her horse in an easy, pretty attitude is looking down at him, a half smile upon her lips, a smile of scorn, and wrath, and something else impossible to understand.

"I don't presume to be sure of anything. I, however, accept your present hint. I only wish you had spoken sooner. To me "—he clears his throat—" Grant seems a very suitable husband for you. I wish you had spoken before. I should certainly have made no objection. If he has not money, he has a profession, and he will get on in it, no doubt, and his family is excellent. I really wish you had let me into your confidence before. For my part I think him a very good fellow. If you had told me before of your lo—affection

——" he stumbles over this unmistakably, but without losing hold of himself altogether. "If you had told me you wished to marry Grant"—here another stumble—"I should, as your guardian—have given you all the help I could."

He stops, he has shifted his gun from one shoulder to the other, and back again, and still is waiting for an answer. Why he should wait is not clear to him. All he knows is that he *is* waiting, and that her answer, when it comes, will mean life or death.

"You are *too* good, *too* kind," the answer comes at last from lips parted, pale, but smiling. The smile is distinctly hostile, and in the eyes dwells hostility too, and something more that goes to Wortley's heart—is it wrath or hatred or—grief?

"But as a fact—you are fond of facts, are you not?—I do not want to marry Captain Grant or Captain Stairs, or—" with a direct glance at him, and with eyes that flame anew, "*anyone*."

A moment later and she is gone.

CHAPTER IX.

"This thought is as a death!"

GONE! Her pretty mare, always a little restive under control, gladly springs forward beneath the touch of his mistress's light hand upon the curb and soon both are racing across field and moor again.

The wild excitement of the gallop falls in well with Nell's present mood, the air flying past her face seems to soothe her, and take from the late passage of arms much of its bitterness. For one thing it leaves her small time for thought, and coming to an old iron gate-way that leads through a once handsome, but now deserted and weed-grown avenue to a magnificent view of the sea, she determines on carrying her ride so far. Yes, she will go up to the top of Lone Crag, and there watch the waves beat their hearts out against the rocks.

Bringing the mare to the gateway, she

bends forward, and tries to lift the latch with the handle of her whip, but Miss Jenkins, restive always, sidles backwards and forwards, preventing her from attaining her object.

However, after two or three ineffectual attempts, she manages to get the gate open in spite of her, and giving it a vigorous push with the handle of her whip, leads the mare through. The push, unfortunately, had been too vigorous—the gate, though old is well-hung, and coming with a crash against the stonework at the other side, swings back again violently against the mare's flank. The latter, irritated no doubt by the many checks during her morning gallop, and never of a very satisfactory temper, becoming thoroughly unnerved by this unexpected shock, rears frantically, plunges forward, rears again—and throws her rider heavily!

There had been one sharp cry—no more. Nell, expecting the reclosing of the gate as little as the mare, had been quite as unprepared for the shock, and the second rear had flung her right out of the saddle—some merciful help from Heaven having loosed her foot from the stirrup. It was all so sudden, that she had hardly time for thought—for fear, and the mare, after that last rear, had bolted, leaving behind her on the moist earth, a slender figure huddled up — senseless — motionless!

Now the last sound of the mad brute's flying hoofs has ceased upon the air. Nothing is here, but silence, deep and lasting. A little frightened hush seems to have fallen upon everything.

"Not a breath crept through the rosy air,
 And yet the fresh leaves seem'd stirr'd with prayer!"

Once a chaffinch, creeping close to the small gloved hand, regards it searchingly, with its head bent to one side—then, as if terrified, flies away—though surely there was small cause for fear in that little lifeless palm. The girl's hat has fallen off, and rolled to some distance from her, and the soft drowsy wind is playing with the curls upon her forehead. One foot is showing beneath the short skirt of her habit, the other is doubled up beneath her. Her pale lips are slightly parted, and the half-closed eyes seem gazing dumbly at the blue heaven above them.

* * * * *

Wortley, when Nell had ridden abruptly from him, had gone on his own way. This, as it chanced, led him by an oblique and much shorter route than she had taken, to the old gate through which she had striven to enter. His thoughts are bitter enough as he goes along, and so engrossing, that the partridges come to no grief at his hands. Perhaps, the bitterest part of his meditations lies in the doubt as to whether his part in the late encounter had been a very manly one. He had purposely offended, and almost insulted her — certainly she had considered herself most unkindly used. Was it all worth while? Could he change her mood— or alter her character? Was this senseless quarrelling to be kept up for ever? And after all, what right had he to——

What is that over there? His thoughts come suddenly to an end. He had just been crossing a stile, and now stands on the topmost rung of it, with all the broad stretch of barren land below him exposed to view. Across it a horse is tearing, saddled, bridled, but riderless.

Great Heaven! it is hers! From where is it coming? He glances rapidly backwards, and from right to left, but nothing is to be seen. Flinging down his gun, he springs to the ground, and dashes across the country towards that part from which the horse had seemed to come. It is a bare chance, but he will use it.

As he runs, he never for a moment deludes himself. He might have relieved his maddening fears, by suggesting to himself that she had dismounted, and when safely on the ground, her horse, frightened at some passing shadow, had bolted; that he would see her presently, and laugh with her over the absurd situation. No. No. He felt he should never laugh with her again—should never scold her again—should never—— Oh! God forgive him!—how could he ever have darkened the smile on that joyous face —should never make her unhappy again!

No hope at all beguiles his way—nothing travels with him but the blackest despair!

Presently he reaches the road, and looks up and down it, breathing heavily, his eyes straining for signs. No, no sight of horse's hoofs anywhere! He was wrong then, the mare had not come up this road. Once again he looks straight down the road, this time, to where in the far distance the old iron gate can be seen.

Ah, *there!* Surely those marks in the dusty road outside the gate mean something. The gate too—is not closed as usual. In there she must have gone. It is a clue, at all events.

It takes him but two minutes to get to the gate—to push it further open, to——

*   *   *   *   *

He has fallen on his knees beside her, and lifted her head on his arm. Oh! Nell! Oh! *Nell!*

The dear little head, all crushed and soiled, and the face, with the beautiful lips and the half-dead eyes, and that terrible smile—so calm—so placid! And the soft hair blown apart!

For a moment Wortley thought he was going mad, and in that moment he knew that he loved her; that he had loved her all along; from the very first instant he had ever seen her. He knew more than that — it seemed quite clear to him in that awful moment, that he would never love a woman again as he had loved her. And she was lying here within his arms—crushed, senseless —perhaps dead!

He lays his hand upon her heart, but for awhile can feel nothing. Then at last it seems to him that some feeble throbbing can be felt. Thrusting his hand into his pocket he searches for his flask—to find nothing there. On most days he has taken a little whisky with him, but this day of all days he has come empty-handed!

Despair again seizes him, and he curses himself aloud as a fool. What *is* to be done? *What?*

Laying her down gently again upon the ground, he strips off his coat, and folding it, lifts her head, and lays it tenderly beneath her as a pillow.

So still, so quiet! He turns away from her, as if hardly daring to look again. Like that— lying there—so might she look if . . . His very flesh seems to shrink. Thrills of misery run through him. *Dead!* She cannot be dead.

Again he bends over her, his cheek to her lips. No breath—no faintest breath. He lays his hand upon her brow, it is cold— colder than before.

He springs to his feet, frenzy seizing him, and looks wildly towards the road. Is there no one? *Can* Heaven forget?

Heaven has not forgotten. Down the road comes a brougham—Mrs. Wilding inside it. The Wildings live just near this old deserted spot. Wortley, forgetful of his shirt sleeves, runs out to intercept it.

"My *dear* Sir Stephen!" cries Mrs. Wilding, thrusting a laughing face out of the carriage window. "Is it a duel—or——?" She has seen his face now, and cries quickly, all her gaiety gone, "Oh! *What* has happened?"

"Come — come!" says Wortley, "Miss Prendergast has been thrown from her horse, and is——" He cannot bring himself to utter the words, "dead—or dying."

Mrs. Wilding opens the door of the brougham—Sir Stephen has forgotten to do it for her — and springs to the ground. Besides what he has said, a glance at his face has told her that something is dreadfully wrong. She follows him quickly to where Nell is lying, a little forlorn figure upon the sweet wild landscape.

Mrs. Wilding who, like many frivolous persons, is *au fond* extremely clever and capable, kneels down beside the prostrate figure, and loosening the clothes on the chest, runs her hand inwards.

"She is warm, and she breathes," she looks up at Wortley, whose face is terrible. "Sir Stephen, you must take the carriage and——" All at once the terror on Wortley's face and the meaning of it becomes clear to her. "No"—rising hurriedly—" you will stay here, and I shall hurry back and get the landau with——"

"No—you stay!" says Wortley vaguely, "I'll——"

"Better not. I can give directions. I shall bring the landau with a stretcher in it, and a mattress, and George. I'll be here in ten minutes."

Sir Stephen lifts to her eyes full of gratitude.

"For God's sake, hurry!" says he hoarsely. "*He* will reward you! I think you are the best woman I ever met."

Mrs. Wilding gets up from her knees, her Parisian skirt extremely muddied, and runs back to the brougham.

"Home! Home!" cries she to the coachman, and presently Wortley finds himself alone again with his little silent companion.

How frightful the silence is! How cold she seems lying there. Unable to bear this thought he lifts her head and holds it against his heart. There it lies immovably—without a knowledge of its resting-place. The thought that if she *were* to know, she would have despised this resting-place, have refused it, adds to the poignancy of the hour! It seems to him as though he is acting dishonourably towards her, is compelling her to accept from him a love she would, if she knew, have scorned. Here she lies in his arms unable to reject—to scorn. . . .

Will she ever be able to see him again? Is life still with her? How still she lies—how horribly quiet! *So* she might lie in her grave clothes—with her eyes shut for the last time!

As though this thought is intolerable he rises, laying her gently back upon his coat, and going to the gateway, stares eagerly with miserable eyes along the road.

Will no one ever come? Ah! there—surely!

CHAPTER X.

" Neither the sun nor death can be looked at steadily."

AT last! At last the sound of wheels! And now the landau is outside the gate, with a stretcher arranged in it from seat to seat, and on it a soft mattress. George Wilding is with his wife this time, and follows her anxiously to where the slender body is lying —still mute as death itself—still utterly unconscious. Mrs. Wilding stooping over her, slips her arm under her neck.

" Now lift her! " says she in a whisper that comes so naturally in the presence of death or disaster of any kind—and Wilding, in obedience to a sign from her, gently inserts his arms beneath the body, near the feet, Wortley making a third part of this human stretcher beneath her waist. With all the tenderness in the world they raise her, but, in spite of their care, a slight groan comes from the poor child they are carrying. Wortley hearing it, turns as white as paper, and casts an agonised glance at Mrs. Wilding.

"No—no," says she hastily, and with the quickest sympathy. "Don't think about that. Thank God rather, that she is *able* to make a sound."

Such hope does she give him, and he gladly catches at it. Indeed, Mrs. Wilding at this painful moment proves the good that is in her, and many of those who are always only too ready to malign her—condemn her as vain and frivolous—might well have been shamed to-day before the strength and humanity she shows.

They have laid Nell upon the mattress now, Mrs. Wilding taking one corner near her, and half kneeling indeed, so as to be of service at any moment. She had compelled Wortley to take the seat opposite to her, understanding in her quick way, that he would not lose sight of the senseless face for even a second if possible. Wilding has sprung up beside the coachman.

"I suppose you thought me dreadfully long," said Mrs. Wilding, glancing up at

Wortley, as the horses go carefully over the road. "It must have seemed horrible to you alone there. But I hurried all I could, and I think I arranged as well as possible under the circumstances. You," *very* kindly, and not looking at him now, "must not be too down-hearted. I feared for her leg, its being twisted beneath her like that—but I am sure it is not broken, and George sent a messenger on horseback to Doctor Bland, so that I think he will be there before us."

They had decided on taking her home at once, a side road that leads to Gaveston Park, being only a quarter of a mile farther than the drive to Wilding's house.

Sir Stephen casts a glance of undying gratitude at her, which after all she does not see; but he never to the day of his death forgets this hour, and the part she played in it!

* * * * *

It is quite dark now. The night has descended. Wortley in the drawing-room at the Park is walking up and down—alone. Dr. Bland had been on the spot when they brought the body home, and a great man from town had come by the six o'clock train, having been telegraphed for. A frightful silence seems to reign over the house, and not even the foot-fall of a servant can be heard here, in this long, gaunt drawing-room.

An hour ago, indeed, a servant had come to ask if he should light the lamps, but Wortley had begged him to let things be as they were—the darkness seemed more supportable than the light, and outside the night was tranquil, and there was a promise of a moon.

It was frightful for all that, waiting here, listening for sounds — wondering what the doctor's verdict would be — unknowing whether life still dwelt in her. A hundred times he had gone to the open door and listened, and twice he had crept half way up the stairs, but no sound came to him—no faintest whisper of a voice, and he had crept down again, haggard, miserable, half mad with suspense.

Now again he goes to the door listening— listening always, but again nothing but this ghastly silence. What are they doing up in that room, with his poor love—his heart's delight—fighting with death? Oh! to know *something*—anything!

Suddenly the thought of going out and standing beneath her window occurs to him. It will be a relief, at all events, it will give him something to do. A few stars are shining now, and the moon's pale radiance is casting shadows amongst the laurels. Here, here is her window; a little light streaming from between the closed shutters, tells him he is right, and breathless, absolutely wretched, he watches it.

All at once a sharp cry reaches him, coming from the room above—a most bitter cry, that dies away into a thrilling shriek. Wortley's heart stands still. For a moment a grip upon it, as of a hand, renders him senseless to all but that fierce, low, agonized cry; but presently he wakes to the fact that it is ended, and that he is standing out here with his hands clenched, and with a fine night wind playing upon the thick moisture on his forehead—moisture born of anguish.

Was that her dying scream? Was it all

over? He went back to the house and through the window again, and so to the door and the hall. Now there were swift goings to and fro upstairs and for a minute the sound of human voices. *The* room, her room was open. Then the door shut again, and all was still. She was not dead, however, so much he knew involuntarily by those muffled sounds above.

Back to the drawing-room again, and to and fro—to and fro. To remain still is impossible. Presently he becomes conscious that something is in the room besides himself, and turning, a most forlorn little boy comes to him, fastening frightened little fingers on his coat.

" Where's Nellie ?—what are they doing to her ? "

It is Geoffrey, neglected and forgotten by the servants.

"God knows, my poor little man," says Wortley, taking him up in his arms, and trying to soothe the broken-hearted sobs that are bursting from the child's heart. Tired-out, hungry and lonely, he is crying as though he would never stop. Presently, however, the sobs grow fewer, and Wortley, still holding him, sits down.

After a while, he knows the child is asleep, but still he holds him in his arms, deriving some strange odd comfort out of his contact with the little slumbering form.

And time goes on—minute added to minute makes the hour. The moon is now quite brilliant, and is pouring its rays through the open windows on to the drawing-room carpet. And now there are footsteps in the hall, uncertain, stumbling. Wortley, his heart beating violently, gets up, and placing the boy upon a sofa, waits for what is yet to come.

The moonbeams light up Cecilia's face as she staggers into the room. Wortley hardly knows her. She leans against the lintel of the door, as if unable to go farther.

"She is alive," she says in a voice unrecognisable, "she will live. But her back. . . . They fear . . . they think . . . she *will never walk* again!"

With a hoarse sob, she sinks upon her knees exhausted, worn-out with grief and horror!

CHAPTER XI.

> "And in my hart also,
>   Is graven with letters depe,
> A thousand sighs and mo,
> A flood of tears to wepe."

THE last remnant of Autumn is gone, and dreary December is well begun. To-day is dismal, and incessant raindrops patter against the window panes, whilst along the garden walks, tiny streams are rushing. No flowers, no sunshine, no blue sky, nothing but scurrying clouds, and passionate showers, and a wind that makes the casements shiver.

There is a roaring fire in the library, and on a lounge close to it lies Nell, in a loose white woollen gown, and a fur rug hung across her feet. Here she lies, day by day, reading or talking to those around her, specially to her slave Geoffrey, who drags all his toys to the side of her sofa, and spends all his indoor hours with her.

Of visitors she has many, though never

too many for her. In some strange, unexpected way, she longs for them, welcomes them—perhaps it is a sad, lingering touch of vitality that makes her cling to the world outside, the world she never sees, that makes her accept thankfully a knowledge of it at second hand. A month ago, she was allowed for the first time to come downstairs, and after that her friends and acquaintances were admitted to see her. Mickey had begged, borrowed or stolen two days from his work in Ireland, to run over and look at her—a bare look indeed, as he arrived one morning and had to leave the same day by the evening train. The meeting between the two, who had quarrelled through their entire friendship, was sad in the extreme, and McNamara returned to Cork more nearly broken-hearted than anyone had ever believed he could be, with his careless, happy-go-lucky nature.

Even the strong-minded Maria was reduced to tears at the first glance at the little pale, mournful face, and had abstained from denunciations for an hour and a half. This might have been because she had filled up that time by explaining to everybody that if she had been on the spot instead of that senseless Stephen, Nell would now be on her feet again, and as well as ever. Better than ever apparently, according to her showing. She had, as usual, a dozen cures for every disease under the sun, and left a sheaf of them with Cecilia for Nell's immediate use. She had been unaffectedly kind and concerned, however, and everyone felt positively kindly disposed towards her when she went.

Mrs. Wilding came very often, always cheery and delightful, but shockingly slangy, and Mrs. Chance had come once. It was impossible to be "nasty" before that pretty, stricken form, and Bella found it hard to be continually "nice", so after that first unavoidable visit, she stayed away—her brother making up for her deficiencies in this line. Yet every visit that Grant paid was pure agony to him, and at last became more than he could endure. His regiment had been ordered home, and was expected next week at Beggars' Bush Barracks in Dublin. He determined to fling up the remainder of his leave and rejoin it there. He had not strength to watch Nell day after day chained to that dreadful sofa—his own sufferings seemed more to him than even hers. The strain was too much for him and he broke down. If there was even a chance of her ever being better. . . .

But that was all over. Hope, indeed, was at an end with all her friends. Even Cecilia, who had fought desperately against the first decision, had now given in, and no longer declared it impossible — *impossible*, that her Nellie would never move about again. Old Dr. Bland, cross-examined by Gaveston, had grown tender beneath the grief of everybody, and had ventured on vague comfort. " *Time* might do something. He had known cases where recovery . . ." Pressed even more anxiously, he had gone on to say, most reluctantly, as it appeared to Cecilia, who was present, that he *had* known two or three people, who, after a similar accident—or as nearly similar as possible — had after six months or a year, recovered the use of their limbs.

"Were those cases *quite* the same as this?"

"Well, no two cases were ever *quite* alike, but there was no such great dissimilarity, but that——"

He broke off there as if unwilling to finish his sentence, and began a new one.

"They must not be too sanguine. Hope was a delusive thing. He had known of a man partially paralysed, on whom an unexpected shock had had the most marvellous results, but such results were rare."

The big man from town, Sir Jefferson Jefferson, had said something nearly the same. Time, time! They must *wait!*

"Miserable comforters were they all." Who was to supply the shock that was to work the miracle? And the shock itself, what terror did it not evoke? Were they to desire evil, that good might come? What could a shock mean to them but further disaster?

* * * * *

Geoffrey has just poked the fire for the third time, at Nell's suggestion—who knows the thrill of fearful joy it gives him to see the sparks fly and the flames dart upwards?—

when the door is thrown open and Wortley is announced.

"What a wet day?" says he cheerfully, coming over to the lounge and taking the small delicate hand extended to him.

"Yes," she looks indifferent. She who used to resent a wet day, as a special grievance to herself—who used to mope in little pretty ways, when it was no longer possible to run through the gardens, or ride through The Park. "You should not have come out."

"One chooses the lesser evil. At home I should have had a dreary day indeed. Here I have you to talk to. Selfish, isn't it?"

Nell looks at him softly.

"Don't you think I know?" says she. "You have come here to-day to make my day a little shorter for me—no more."

"There is something more certainly. To make my own day a little shorter too. I am sorry for your sake that it is so dark and wet."

"It is all the same to me," says she, still indifferently. Her head is lying on her palm, her eyes gazing into the glowing fire. Geoffrey on the hearthrug is building castles out of bricks.

Wortley makes her no reply, for the moment indeed, reply is beyond him. That little form on the sofa, so still, so resigned—so humbly resigned.

It is her resignation that touches him most. Her utter giving in to her cruel fate! Could three months, three bare months have so changed any human thing? Where is the laughter now, that used to make gay the lovely eyes—where is the quick return, the saucy answer? The lovely eyes are quiet now—he can hardly bear the quiet of them—and her whole manner is so changed, and sadly changed, that scarcely he recognises it. Yet the change has not brought bitterness with it, or discontent, or wild regret, or angry rebellion against Heaven.

It has been known of some of the most perfect creatures that this poor earth can produce that, taken from a happy state, to grief and ill-health; some of the finer feelings fell from them in their great stress—that the quick change from life to a living death, had broken down their strongholds, and destroyed their fortresses and given them over to the enemy, bringing them even to a lower level than those, who (before Fate spoke) had been so sadly their inferiors in every way. Yet this poor child, who had aspired to nothing, has seemed to gather from her grief and pain only the sweetest graces.

The little petulant moods, that were only half meant always, where are they now? The angry shrug, the frowning glances. Gone! All gone!

A sharp sigh breaks from Wortley. Oh, that they were all back again.

"What are you thinking of?" Her voice breaks into his thoughts. The evening has lowered greatly since his coming, and only the splendid blazing of the fire lights up the room.

"Many things. And you?"

"You don't deserve to have your question answered. And yet—I will tell you. I was thinking of long ago, and that you need not have scolded me so very badly about my behaviour to Captain Grant, after all. You remember, don't you?"

"Did I scold you?" says he, a little choking sensation in his throat.

"You did," she turns from him with a touch of the old petulance. "And so uselessly too! You won't have to scold me any more. I couldn't marry him now even if I wanted to."

Wortley does not answer her. His anguish is too great for words. Getting up, he walks to the window, and stares with unseeing eyes into the growing blackness of the night.

"Come back," cries the soft voice penitently. "Oh, I'm sorry, I'm sorry." There are tears in the voice now. " I shouldn't have said that. And I meant nothing, *really*. Only you didn't understand me once. Come back, and forgive me."

"Forgive you!" His tone is heart-broken. He would have come back to her at once, but a sense of shame forbids him to let her see the tears that are standing thick within his eyes—he who could not remember crying since his mother's death, and he was then such a little fellow.

"Come here," says Nell. And then miserably—"Oh, you ought to come. You know I can't go to you." This sad reproach brings him to her at once. "And I was wrong, I acknowledge it. I shouldn't have said it. You *will* come . . . . Stephen."

It is the first time she has ever called him by his Christian name, and it seems to add another pang to the moment. To Wortley, who knows the proud, spoilt nature of her, it is plain that she must indeed have made it clear to herself that henceforth no man can woo or wed her—that love is dead to her—before she thus addressed him.

"I am here," says he, bending over her. "But as for forgiveness, Nell, what is there to forgive? It is I who should go on my knees to you. That last day, just before . . . I would to God I had been dead before I said what I did to you that day."

"There—there—there now," says she, putting up her hand and taking his. "I told myself you would think about that. And what was there to think about after all? You gave me a good scolding, which I resented— but which I well deserved, all the same."

Wortley with the hand she has given him clasped in both his, feels his grief grow keener. This sad submission, how unlike it is to the demeanour of the angry, defiant child who had ridden away from him on Miss Jenkins' back, who had scorned his authority?

Nell glancing up sees the anguish on his face.

"Oh, I *wish* I hadn't vexed you like this. How selfish I am—saying just what I want to say without thinking. Do you know," beckoning him to come round, with eager fingers, until he is again beside her, on the hearthrug, "I have to fight all day long against this selfishness? I often with my complainings make Cissy and the others unhappy. And that"—leaning towards him—"is unfair, you know, because neither Cecilia, nor Peter have made me a——"

She throws herself back suddenly, and crushes her eyes with her hands.

"Oh! To say it," cries she in a strangled

voice. "But I *will!*" passionately. "I must! —I must learn to say it. A cripple! . . . a cripple! That's what I am."

Wortley's heart seems to stand still. How is he to comfort her? How! As he waits —a little form pushes past him. Geoffrey amidst his bricks had heard that cruel cry, and has run to his auntie and flung himself upon her breast.

"Nellie—Nellie—Nellie!" cries he, clinging to her. "Don't cry—don't. I love you. I do!"

Oh, dear little arms!

CHAPTER XII.

" How bitter and winterly waxed last night
 The air that was mild!
How nipped with frost were the flowers last night,
 That at dawning smiled !
How the bird lost the tune of the song last night,
 That the spring beguiled ! "

SIR STEPHEN had wisely left her alone with the child, and gone home with an insufferable pain at his heart. He had meant to wait until Cecilia's return—who had gone to pay a long-promised and expected visit to a neighbour, ten miles away—but he felt that the child would do his poor little sweetheart more good than he could. He had hoped to sit with her until Cecilia's return, but it seemed impossible.

At this moment Cecilia, springing from her carriage, runs hurriedly up the steps to the hall door, anxious to get back to Nell as quickly as possible. It was against her will she had gone to pay that visit so far away, and she had been fretting all the drive home at the length of time that had elapsed since last she saw Nell. Cecilia's devotion to the poor little sufferer had been marked, and was full of an affection so strong and lasting, as to astonish those who, not unnaturally, had arranged her character for her as a frivolous creature, a coquette, or perhaps something worse; at all events, one whose feelings would always be but skin-deep, mere surface work.

Just inside the hall door, she finds Grant talking to the butler.

"Oh, it is you, Mrs. Gaveston," says he eagerly. "Can I see Miss Prendergast, even for a few minutes? It is late, I know, but——"

"It is six o'clock," says Cecilia gently. "She is often a little tired at this hour. Is it . . . . *Need* you see her just now?"

"I must. I"—with agitation—"I have decided on throwing up the rest of my leave, and rejoining. There"—brokenly—"is no use in my staying here."

"No," says Cecilia. She feels sorry for

him. "If I let you see her, you will be careful, you will not distress her, unnerve her in any way? You know we have always to be very anxious about her." Cecilia does not know of Wortley's late visit, or the agitation arising out of it, or she would have sent Grant away without hesitation, in spite of her pity for him.

"I shall take care. You *know*"—miserably—"I should do that. And I should not have come now but that I, at the last moment, decided on going to-morrow."

"That is sudden, surely!"

"No! I have felt for days that—I could not stay here."

"For days!" Cecilia looks at him. "I *wish* you could have arranged to bid her good-bye in the morning, when she has more strength," says she. "Still, as you are going to-morrow . . . . ." He follows her, but at the door of the library, she motions him to stay there. Going swiftly into the room herself, she bends over Nell, and kisses her fondly. Nell is quite composed again, and lying on her cushions with the faint light from a rose-shaded lamp upon her face, looks singularly well. No traces of her late tears are evident.

"Alec Grant wants to see you, Nellie darling—just for a minute or two. I said he might come in, if you feel well enough to see him."

"He can come," says Nell, indifferently, " but don't let him stay long. Hurry off with your things and come down, I want to hear about your visit. They were at home, of course. And Tilly—what of her?"

"Wants a strait waistcoat worse than ever! I shan't be long. But"—whispering—"I fancy Alec wants to see you alone! He "—in a lower whisper—" is going."

"Going!" startled.

"Yes, away. To rejoin his regiment. He seems in great grief. I tell you to prepare you."

"*Ordered* to rejoin?"

"No, I think not. His own wish. If you would rather not see him, a little note would——"

"I shall see him," says Nell.

Cecilia goes into the hall, leaving the door open for Grant to enter the room, then closes it behind him.

Going over to the couch, he looks down at Nell, with pale face, and working lips. He is no coward where physical matters are concerned, he had indeed distinguished himself in Burmah, where riots among the natives—often very dangerous—had arisen, but he was not strong enough to endure the sight of this hopeless, lingering grief, even though his endurance might tend to alleviate it. He fell short a little, there.

"She has told me," says Nell, delicately anxious to spare him further pain. The distress on his face is terrible. "You are going. You feel that you must go."

"Oh, it is that," says he. He falls on his knees beside her, and takes her hand, such a ridiculously small hand now, and presses his face down upon it. "I can't bear to look at you. It breaks my heart." Some strange revulsion in the girl's mind, here compels her to make an attempt to restore her hand to her own keeping, but he, in a fatuous way, clings to it. "It is killing me. I must go, I must! And yet, life without you . . . . Oh! how miserable I am!"

He stops for a moment, and Nell waits patiently, if a little contemptuously. How like a weak girl it all is! Are some men like girls? A sudden thought coming to her, is as good as an answer. *All* men certainly are not.

"I am going. Our fellows are in Dublin now. I have come to bid you good-bye. I am going to-morrow."

His voice breaks. He loves her very honestly in his own way, but his grief has proved too much for him. He is anxious to hurry away, and leave it behind him. He has no suspicion of selfishness connected with his going, he feels himself indeed the aggrieved person. If Providence had left Nell whole and sound, he would have loved her to his dying day, so he tells himself, but Nell, not whole and sound, how is he to love her? Lying there upon the sofa, crushed, beautiful, incapable of movement. . . . . If life were treble its length, could he ever hope to marry her?

To the poor child lying on the sofa, his quick decision to go—to leave her—is very bitter. He had loved her in her sunny hours, when all the world was bright, and she the brightest thing in all his world—but now laid low and desolate, he shrank from her. He gave her up!

That seems the meaning of it! And the meaning of it really is that life is over for her, that the end of it has reached her before the beginning. She feels forsaken—left here to die or live as Heaven may decree—but of no consequence in the meantime to anyone.

"You are right, quite right," says she, in a stifled tone. "Here you are only wasting your time."

"Ah, you mustn't put it like that," says Grant. "Could I waste time with you? But to see you like this!" He bends his head again upon her hand; and again she feels the hand grow wet. Yet no tears stand in her own sad eyes. "Oh, my darling, that it should be all over. That life should end, like this!"

The words, fraught with real pain, strike

cold to her heart. *Is* it all over—*all;* the sweetness, the beauty of life? Shall she never stand again? or walk from the table over there to the bookcase, or pluck a flower, or chase Geoffrey round the rose-beds! Oh, God. *Dear* God! have mercy!

Grant's words have revived all the terrible resistance against her fate, that for the past months has been troubling her. She had fought, and told herself she had overcome, but now this open desertion of her, this casting of her aside as a derelict on life's ocean, has raised from the dead her buried agony.

Is she to be a living corpse for years and years, and years!

His face is crushed against her hand, so that the strange lights and shades upon her face are unknown to him. In five minutes she has gone through a very hell of misery— a hell made worse by the fact that she has to endure it without movement of any kind. Oh! all of you, who can rise and walk; think of the relief it is to be able to go to and fro at certain times—to pace a floor—to push a chair aside—to—maybe, smash in pieces a fan—or a branch—to be able to *leave* a room.

Then all at once her pain grows less. Her eyes lighten, and a little suspicion of disdain comes into them. The disdain helps her. A scene has come back to her—a happy brilliant scene where the man—now kneeling at her side, with her hand clasped in his, and weeping over the fact that he must leave her, because of the grievous ill that has befallen her—stood and told her, in the bright summer sunshine, summer words.

"It would be great glory to die for you."

The words come back now, and a pale smile lights her lips as she repeats them. To *die* for her when he cannot even *live* for her —when he must needs leave her because the very sight of her, distresses him beyond endurance. "That life should *end* like this." It is he who has elected to make an end.

The fact that she has never felt for Grant anything more than a girlish friendship, does not lighten the bitterness of his desertion of her in her need.

"You are going then," says she presently. "Your regiment has come back, Cecilia tells me. You are going—where?"

"To Ireland—to Dublin. It is not so far away. Perhaps some time—— When I am quite well?" Her laugh rings a little hollow. "Yes; you must come back then. In the meantime, I am glad you are going back to your duties—you are very wise."

She smiles at him from under the hand she has laid over her eyes. But the smile contains many hidden things.

He is forsaking her in her trouble, before his duties compel him to do so, and such forsaking seems cruel to her. She had never cared for him in any way, yet this open forsaking of her, cuts to the poor child's very soul! She is of no use at all, it seems! No longer will *anyone* find pleasure in her.

Grant has not the first place in these despairing thoughts; and yet the one who *has* that place is, with a determination worthy of an older and stronger mind— pushed deliberately aside.

She is cast adrift—a bit of the flotsam and

jetsam that lie for ever drifting here and there upon the waters of life—a poor little crushed bit of timber that no one would care to drag to land.

"It is not wisdom," says Grant at last. "It is misery! I shall think of you, and you always. I shall never," with dismal conviction, "think of anyone else if I lived —for ever."

"That's a long time," says Nell, with a wretched little smile. "Does anyone live for ever? I hope *I* shall not. And as you *are* going to Ireland?—well, then, go."

"Nell—what a last word."

"I'll improve on it. Go—in peace."

"I shall go in sorrow," says he, breaking down again, and then, slowly—very unhappily —"Nell, may I kiss you?"

"No." Swiftly she lays her hands across her lips; there is even terror in her action.

Grant rises to his feet.

"Not even so much."

"I cannot."

She has taken down the right hand, but still keeps the left across her lips.

"You never loved me," says he.

There is no answer.

He moves to the door.

"But—I liked you," cries she. It is a most miserable little apology.

* * * * *

Entering his sister's house twenty minutes later, Grant finds her in her tiny drawing-room.

"It is over," says he. "All over!!" The dull misery in his face does not touch her sufficiently to prevent her reply.

"I'm glad of it," says she. "It is just as well as it is, Alec, believe me. You would never have been happy with her. She is a most undesirable person. I detested her from the first, though I never *said so.*"

"She is the last person on earth to be detested by anybody," says Grant hotly. "She is——"

"Yes?" derisively.

"The very first person to be admired by everybody! Why," turning upon her angrily, "you used to think her perfection when I first came here. You saw no fault in her then."

"Not *then*," says Mrs. Chance, smiling her curious smile. "You could have *married* her then! But now! I could have endured her for your sake—because she might have helped you in your career ; but I always hated her. She was antagonistic to me in every way, but you know the old lines :

" ' O, what a world of vile ill-favour'd faults
 Looks handsome in three hundred pounds a year.'

Her 'three hundred pounds a year' would have been very useful to you."

"I had forgotten that she ever had a penny," says Grant. "I'd have married her gladly without one, but for this awful misfortune that has befallen her."

"I daresay ; there are always fools in the world," says his sister with a shrug.

CHAPTER XIII.

"This bitter love is sorrow in all lands.
Draining of eyelids, wringing of drenched hands,
Sighing of hearts and filling up of graves."

CHRISTMAS has come and gone, that saddest time of all the year for those whose hearts are weary, and a New Year has dawned. A New Year that seems to have little prospect of happiness in it for those at Gaveston Hall!

It is still early in January, and Cecilia going listlessly up the grand old oaken staircase, pauses at different niches to notice with a half-hearted admiration the glorious pots of chrysanthemums standing in them. Tall and stiff they hold themselves—bronze and white and cream, but, for the most part, deepest yellow—with a view, no doubt, to lighting up the staircase. Erect and stately they salute her as she goes by—a golden glory in the misty darkness of the lamp-light.

Cecilia stops to pat their lovely faces, and to

gaze into their golden hearts. She seems glad to stop now and then. Her step is heavier than it used to be, and something of the old glad light has passed from her eyes for ever. Her smile, too, is less ready, and when it comes—unwillingly always—it is as sad as tears.

A clock downstairs striking the hour, rouses her from her contemplation of the chrysanthemums. Five o'clock. Not later than that? There are sounds of coming storm in the air, and the light of heaven has been darkened even earlier than usual on this winter night. So early, that the servants have seen fit to supplant it by lights of earthlier mould.

Cecilia, hastening her footsteps, goes farther up the stairs, then pauses again to look through a window into the sullen blackness of the night.

All day—all day her thoughts have been with Phil. Fight with them, conquer them as she will, they rise, even half-slain, to challenge her again. Now they are enveloping her in on every side, and fresh battle must be done before she goes on to Nell, who to-night is lying in her boudoir—Nell, who has been a little capricious, a little restless of late—to whom change seems positively necessary, be it only from room to room.

Presently Cecilia, having cast her particular Satan again behind her, goes in languidly to where she knows Nell is expecting her. As she reaches the door, a servant overtakes her, a telegram in his hand. There was no answer, the man said. Cecilia, taking it, idly and without interest, enters her pretty boudoir, where Nell is lying, with a book and a shaded reading-lamp on a small table near her. The room is bright with flowers and lights, and the gay crackling of a roaring fire.

"A telegram?" says she, with some interest, as Cecilia stoops over her to kiss her. It has seemed to Cecilia lately that she can never kiss her enough. Dear Nell! Poor—*poor* Nell!

"Yes. How are you now, darling? Not too tired?"

"Not tired at all. And this book is charming." She lays down "The Little Minister" as she speaks, somewhat reluctantly. "But your telegram! Is there anything in the world so exciting as a telegram? Open it. It may be important."

Mrs. Gaveston laughs, glad at the quick interest she takes in it.

"Important, and to *me*?"

"Why not to you?"

"'A woman of *no* importance?' Well—here it is." She opens it with careless fingers. "I always look at the name first. The message is always a poor thing next to that."

Her eyes are on the pink paper now—*on the name!*

Suddenly she throws up her head as if mortally wounded, and her fingers close convulsively on the bit of paper—reducing it to a crushed ball. Now she turns her eyes on her sister.

"Cissy—what is it?" cries Nell terrified.

"He is dying."

"He?" Nell, although she asks the question, *knows*.

"Phil! He is dying!"

She looks dazed—like one hardly understanding. Then suddenly a fit of shivering catches hold of her. "Dying—dying!"

As if the repetition of the awful word has caused a revulsion of feeling, she all at once grows calm again.

"It isn't true. Of course"—with emphasis—"it isn't true. But I must go to him."

"*Go?*"

"Yes. Yes. Yes. Now, not a word, Nell. I shall go, though you, and Peter, and the whole world held me."

"Go where? Give me that telegram?"

"He is at Burnley." She had had only one glance at the telegram, but every letter in it seems burned into her brain. Burnley is ten miles from Bigley-on-Sea. "He is dying at Burnley. And he has asked me to go to him." She is standing, white, rigid, looking before her, with a curious light in her eyes, as though they are looking at something beyond the wall that bounds her gaze.

"*How* can you go?" says Nell.

"I shall go."

"But——"

"It is useless, Nell."

"Oh! no! You will listen! You will,

darling." Seeing Cecilia's utter indifference to her words, she loses her head a little. "Oh! dear, *dear* Heaven, why am I chained here, why can't I help her?" She beats her hands frantically against her breast. "Cissy —listen—*listen*."

What had she meant to say? In her terrible agitation she forgets everything, and sinks back exhausted against her pillows.

"I shall go," repeats Cecilia slowly, firmly. To Nell she appears taller in some strange way, and singularly decided. It is doubtful if she has even heard the girl's passionate appeal. Her eyes are still staring straight before her, and now there is a tragic look in them. If her face is cold and white, it is still quite composed, and she stands erect, disdaining, as it were, even to rest her hand upon the chair near her. She feels strong, determined. Everything seems blotted out from her, save the fact that she must go to Phil, and soon—at once. Even Nell is forgotten, as, with a quick step, she turns and leaves the boudoir.

In her bedroom she unclasps her hand, and

pulling out the telegram into readable form again, looks at it.

"I am dying. Come to me."

So terse—so plain—and yet filled with an agony unbearable. "Come to me." Yes, she will go to him, though it cost her her life, and all that makes life dear. Once she had refused to go with him, now—what shall keep her from him? The paper lying in her hand seems to burn itself into her palm. *Dying!*

For a long, long time she stands motionless. Then suddenly, as if recollecting the passing of time, she slips the telegram into her bosom, and going to her wardrobe, pulls out, with feverish haste, a cloak, a hat, and some furs. She has made no plans up to this—she is so accustomed to have all her plans arranged for her, that she has forgotten to make any—but now the fact is forced upon her that she will have to give orders. A carriage will be wanted—and——

How is she to get away without Peter's

knowledge? That seems easy enough. Peter is in the library, lost amongst his newspapers, and will be blind and deaf to everything until the dressing-bell rings. There is plenty of time. She will be gone before he knows anything.

"Gone! before he knows. He will know when she *is* gone!

She drops the cloak she is holding, and a frown gathers on her forehead. He will know—and he will think——

Oh! what does it matter what anyone thinks? There is only one thing to remember now. Phil is dying, and has sent for her.

She picks up the cloak again, and throws it over her shoulders, and hurriedly covers her head with a little soft felt hat, and moves towards the bell. With her hand on it, she pauses.

To go like this—to steal out of the house without a word, a sign. She has not loved him as he might have been loved, but he has always been very good to her. Shall she face him—acknowledge all—then leave him?

No—a thousand times *no!* She takes her hand from the bell, and clutching at the mantelpiece, sways a little, her breath coming quickly, unevenly. To tell him—to see his eyes as she tells him. Never! Death would be better than that. She tells herself she knows him well enough to be quite sure that there would be no forgiveness for her, were they both to live a hundred years. He must think what he will of her. She can never tell him. Never!

And with this she finds herself moving towards the door, and down the staircase, and straight into the library where he is sitting, with the *Morning Post* before him.

As he hears her approaching footsteps, he turns his head slowly to greet her, as he ever greets her, with his tender smile. But one glance at her brings him to his feet.

"Good Heavens! What has happened?" exclaims he.

Her face is white and terribly changed.

"I have come to tell you something," says she, slowly—coldly, as though feeling in her is benumbed.

CHAPTER XIV.

" There is no certainty in happiness."

AND then she told him! Deliberately, almost callously, in a low, monotonous tone that had ceased to be hers. He hardly recognized it, or her either. He listened, though without a comment, without a movement, save that once he laid his hand heavily upon the back of his chair, and tightened his grasp there until his knuckles showed white. His self-control was superb, and if she could have been impressed by anything in that awful hour, she would have been impressed by it.

The low, dull voice went on with its miserable declaration—a confession, or whatever it was—and he lost not one word of it, though through it all, he felt his whole life crumbling to dust beneath his feet. There was nothing left—nothing to hold by, to cling to, to save it from total wreckage. He felt suddenly old, so old, that he wondered if he had ever been young! And he had been so *sure*—so certain—so carelessly happy in his fool's paradise.

Had ever man been so befooled before? Had he been blind, deaf, *dead*, that he could not see? He had noticed that she had been a little depressed of late, but he had put it down to ill-health, and had implored her to see Bland, and Bland had assured him that once the winter was over, she would pick up again. It was nothing, he said.

Nothing!

Cecilia's new voice has ceased, and silence falls upon the room . . . through it, some lines he had read somewhere some time ago, seem to ring, beating feebly at his heart.

> " My days are in the yellow leaf,
> The flowers and fruits of love are gone.
> The worm, the canker, and the grief,
> Are mine alone."

If he had but known it, these last were his only possessions for many months. Love, blind fool! he had dreamed of love! and where is it now, that dream? And life—what does life hold for him? Love is life—the beginning and the end thereof—and love has not once come nigh him.

He had not looked at her during her terrible revelation; nor she at him. Now he rouses to the fact of the continued silence, and all at once a mad fancy that it is not true, that he is sleeping, that he will wake soon to laugh at his hideous fears, gives him a false strength. He turns abruptly and looks at her, and that one look wakes him indeed. Is that Cecilia! That white, wild-eyed woman! Where is the pretty girl he used to know?

It is all true then. There is no doubt anywhere.

> "Not poppy nor mandragora,
> Nor all the drowsy syrups of the world"

could deaden him to his knowledge of the truth.

"That is all," says Cecilia, disturbed from her reverie by that swift glance of his at her. "I must go." She pulls her cloak round her with a shiver.

"Not quite all, I think!" His tone is even.

"You say he asked you—when here, in my house—to go away with him."

"Yes."

"Well?"

"I have told you. I refused to go."

"Why?"

"I—" she hesitates as if thinking. Then says indifferently, "I could not."

"But why?" persistently.

"I could not leave the child."

At this, Gaveston gives way to a sharp, dry laugh that seems to rend him.

"You actually thought of him. Oh! the good mother!"

His tone startles her, it is so unlike Peter to be sarcastic, or bitter, or anything—save kind.

"Yes, I thought of the child. I could not forget him."

"And the child's father"—he moves a step nearer to her—"how was it with him? Did you forget him?"

His eyes are searching hers; there is a sort of cold fury in them. It shakes her. She had never seen him thoroughly roused before, and this man, with the piercing gaze, and the air of splendid disgust, seems unknown to her. It is as though she is now looking at her husband for the first time. She compels herself to answer him.

"Oh! I thought of you too. You"—she stops for a moment, growing agitated—"you had been good to me."

"Had I? It was very good of *you* to remember that insignificant fact. You acknowledge I was good to you then?"

His mocking, contemptuous air, restores her composure more than all his endearments could have done.

"Too good for me to betray you, at all events," says she, the softness gone from her voice.

There is a pause, and then:

"So you wouldn't betray me——"

The cold fury has now warmed into life, his nostrils are dilated. Going up to her, he seizes her by the arms.

"Betrayal! What is betrayal? That devil—did he ever kiss you?"

"Yes; once."

"Once—twice—twenty times."

In his mad passion his fingers tighten on her arms, bruising into the soft flesh—the arms that but an hour ago, he would have killed himself to spare one pang. Perhaps in her own excitement she does not feel the pain, but whether or no, she bears it without flinching.

"Once," she repeats firmly; "believe me or not as you will."

"Once, or twice—what does it matter?" says he, loosening his grasp, and flinging her from him. "Once was contamination enough. And so"—here he looks at her with a glance that must have blighted her, had not her heart been filled with the face of another. "He held you in his arms and kissed you—this man who was as my friend, who accepted my hospitality, who took my hand in his, who dwelt beneath my roof! You ought truly to be proud of your lover—but, had I been in his place—I should, at least, have tried to be a gentleman."

She turns upon him fiercely.

"He was a gentleman! It was I—*I* who persuaded him to accept your invitation here. I made him accept it. And you"—passionately—"how could *you* have been in his place? How could *you* be my lover—you whom I never loved?"

It is a cruel stab, born of a cruel moment. . . . . Again the walls of the room have opened wide, and beyond, dying, lies her lover, waiting—waiting!

"I must go," cries she wildly, turning away.

"One moment!" says Gaveston.

His voice vibrating with a meaning she does not understand, arrests her attention.

She turns.

"I would know one thing more—I would fill up the picture. That once you speak of —*you* . . . kissed *him?*"

She returns his gaze unflinchingly.

At this moment she tells herself she hates him.

"Yes," cries she defiantly. "I kissed him too—I am as bad as he is, he is no worse than I am." It seems to give her a strange delight to make herself as guilty as the man she loves. "But once, once only! Oh!" Suddenly, sharply she lifts her hands, and pressing them convulsively against her eyes, breaks into bitter, dry-eyed sobbing. "Once. Once only. And now he is dying. Oh, Phil! Oh, my love. My love!"

Her strange weeping shakes her slender frame. Her dry sobs come slowly, heavily. There is poignant anguish in them.

Gaveston, as though maddened by the sound, lays his hands upon her shoulders, holding her as in a vice.

"Be silent," orders he sternly. "Have you *no* shame?"

"None. None—where he is concerned." Even whilst he holds her she looks back at him with wild but sad defiance. "I am neither sorry, nor ashamed!"

"That is enough," says he. He releases her quietly. He has grown calm again, with a calmness that chills her more than all his anger had done. "If you are going you had better start at once. Shall I ring the bell for the carriage? By-the-bye, you quite understand what this journey means?"

"Quite."

"It will hopelessly imperil your reputation."

She bows her head.

"And your son?"

"Oh, my God!" cries she suddenly. Her face changes from its icy immobility to a quick agony. "But"—wildly—"he will know — he will understand . . . ."

"You are right. He will certainly understand."

She looks at him with miserable eyes. Too proud to entreat, she stands before him a picture of despair.

"You will tell him?"

"The world will tell him. I"—coldly—"should be the last to speak to my son of his mother's dishonour."

"There was no dishonour."

"We must leave that to the world too. A pitiless judge."

"But the child—the child! *You* know— *you* will tell him—you believe me, Peter—I see by your eyes that you do. *You* will tell him! You will have pity on him."

" I shall have pity on him!" The storm of his rage has died away, and Cecilia, with her dark eyes fixed on his, sees something in his plain, rugged face—something that might be called nobility. Her eyes fall—conscience-stricken she hangs her head. " If you will go," says he—he waits, as if perhaps in this last hour, hoping she will still see where her duty lies—but answer there is none—" I shall go with you."

" *You?* "

" I told you I should have pity on my son. He shall not, if I can prevent it, redden at the mention of his mother's name. Make no further delay"—there is an undisguised touch of scorn in his tone—" if you are ready—so am I. Let us get this thing over as soon as possible."

" It is to shield me," stammers she. " It is kind——"

He checks her peremptorily.

" Enough!" says he brusquely — with almost cruel contempt — turning to ring the bell. "I am thinking only of the boy!"

* * * * *

The carriage is ordered. Five minutes will bring it round. Cecilia has run upstairs once again to her room where Nell in an agony of suspense is waiting.

"I have come to bid you good-bye."

The tragic look is still in her eyes, now augmented by weariness. It seems to Nell that the farewell has something of the eternal in it. She makes a sudden involuntary effort—the effort of one who would rise and go with her, and then with a groan remembering, she sinks back again, covering her face with her hands.

"Peter is going with me," says Cecilia stonily. "I have told him."

"Told him?"

"All!"

"And——?"

"There is no and. It is all over! I knew it would be, when I made up my mind to tell him. You remember once I said to you that Peter was a man who would never forgive. But "—slowly—" what I did not know was, that when the time came, I should not care!" She walks towards the window and looks out. "Oh!" stamping her foot, "will that carriage never come round?"

"Peter is going with you!" Nell repeats this as if stunned—it is as though she has heard, without taking in, anything else. "Peter knows!"

"Oh, yes—yes!" impatiently. "What does it matter? What does anything matter?" She pulls the curtains aside, again gazing out into the fast darkening night. "How long they are!" She beats lightly, irritably upon the sash of the window with her small, closed hand, as if half-maddened by the delay.

Nell—faint, trembling, drags herself a little, upwards—slowly, painfully—clutching at the side of the sofa to help herself. So engrossed is she with fears for Cecilia, that it is not until afterwards, when pain has made her fall back into her original recumbent position— she remembers, that it is the first time for four months that she has unaided raised herself from her pillows.

"You must see," she says—"you cannot *fail* to see"—eagerly—"Peter's goodness in this matter! Oh, Cissy—it is not yet too late——"

The last two words fall like a death-knell on Cecilia's ear.

"Too late!" repeats she wildly. "You are right. I shall be too late. He will die, and not know that I was coming! Oh, Phil! . . . What—*what* can be keeping them? Perhaps"—she turns a wan face on Nell, "perhaps"—with awful suspicion—"Peter—has forbidden—the servants. . . . Nell—if that should be so. . . ."

"You must be mad to think that!" says Nell. It is at this point the pain grows overwhelming and she falls back again upon her cushions. "Peter——" the words come in little gasps—"is indeed a stranger to you. He is . . . incapable of . . . ."

A sound from Cecilia breaks in upon her hurried breathing.

"At last. At last!" cries she feverishly.

The sound of wheels outside can be heard, and in a moment the carriage passes beneath the window, on the way to the hall door. She rushes to the door.

"Cissy, wait one moment," says Nell desperately—she holds out her hands with an imploring gesture.

"There is so little time," says Cecilia. She comes back however.

"Just one promise," says Nell. "Whatever happens. . . . *Whatever* happens—whether he lives or dies—promise me you will come back with Peter."

Cecilia breaks into a strange laugh. It is so reckless that it terrifies Nell.

"You should ask Peter to promise to bring me back," says she. "Haven't you heard me. Have you not understood? Peter will not forgive."

"He will bring you back if you will come."

"Are you so sure?" she smiles coldly. "There"—turning—"I must go!"

"Kiss me then," says poor Nell, sobbing. "My darling—my own sister." She holds up her arms, and Cecilia bends to her. Almost their lips have met, when Cecilia, seeing the pale, pure, now almost spiritual face beneath her, suddenly recoils.

"No!" says she; she pushes back the girl's arms as though dreading them, and in another moment has left the room.

CHAPTER XV.

> " And saying so, the tears out of her eyes
> Fell without noise and comforted her heart.
> Yea, her great pain eased of the sorest part
> Began to soften in her sense of it."

WORTLEY riding home from the meet at a rather unusual pace, stops in a bare space to look at his watch by the light of the rising moon. Of late—ever since Nell's accident—he has fallen into the habit of going to see her every day—in the early afternoon, or else in time for tea. His watch tells him that he will be late for that—it is after six o'clock.

The meet had been at Tor's Place—a long distance from home, and to-day of all days the fox, an old dog-fox of considerable experience—had led them a run of twenty miles or so across a very stiff country. It is rather late to go on to Gaveston Park. Still to see her —that seems important.

He has long ago ceased to deny to himself that his one absorbing emotion in life is Nell. She—and she only—holds his heart in her two hands, and to keep away from her is difficult.

There is still a good hour before dinner, and ten minutes will take him there; he might get a glimpse of her, and then ride home. It seems impossible to wait until to-morrow for that glimpse.

He turns his horse's tired head towards the bye-road that leads to the Park.

Mrs. Gaveston was not at home, the man told him—that surprised him a little, as Cecilia had refused all invitations to dinner of late, all invitations of any kind indeed—a fact laid down by everyone to her affection for her sister—and at this hour where could she have gone except to dine with people some distance from home? It is still early. He hesitates, hardly knowing what to do, and then finally the man decides the matter for him.

"Miss Prendergast is still up, sir."

Wortley nods and goes up to Cecilia's

sitting-room, where he has often before this, seen Nell.

"So your sister has deserted you," says he gaily, as he enters, but one glance at her checks him, and renders him suddenly grave. Lying there in her soft draperies, so pale, so wan, with the traces of tears still wet upon her cheeks, she makes a woeful picture, indeed.

"What is it?" he asks hurriedly. "What is the matter? You are lonely. They should not——"

"No. No." She tries to hide her face from him with her hand, running it nervously over her eyes, as if to shut out the light; and Wortley, divining her desire to be as little seen as possible, takes the lamp nearest her, and carries it to a distant table. "Something dreadful has happened," she says, trying vainly to check her emotion, and speak naturally. "Cecilia—we—have just had a telegram from—to say—poor Philip Stairs is dying."

"Dying—good Heavens! A telegram from where?"

"From Burnley!"

"I thought he was abroad somewhere! Burnley; why, that is only ten miles from here. I passed it to-day."

"Yes; he is there. It must have been some horrible accident, I suppose; but we know nothing. Isn't it all dreadful?" beginning to cry again. "And Cissy—we—it has been a great shock to us. We were both of us very fond of him."

"I know he was a *quite* old friend of yours and Mrs. Gaveston's," says Wortley at once. "I hope she——"

"She has gone to him," in a low tone. Wortley can hardly restrain his glance of surprise.

"Peter has taken her," quickly. "He understands what a friend he was of ours. I was so glad," turning nervously away, "that they both went."

"Yes. It was much better, and just what one would have expected from Gaveston," says Wortley gravely, as befits the occasion, and without an atom of any further meaning. He rises, however, and begins to pace to and fro, the flickering firelight gleaming on his somewhat mud-bespattered breeches, and the red of his coat. Most men look well in their hunting clothes, and Wortley, a plain-featured man in reality, looks very nearly handsome to-night in his—so tall, so strong, so reliable. He also looks very grave, with his hands holding his whip behind his back, and his eyes bent upon the hearth-rug, where he has now come to a stand. All that gossip then was true! Good Heavens! what a situation! How will Gaveston take it—afterwards?

"Was the message very urgent?" asks he presently.

"Very. 'I am dying.'" She cannot bring herself to repeat the rest of it. That "Come to me" was so fraught with unmistakable meaning. "We had no idea he was in the country." Not for a moment does she doubt Cecilia about this; and, indeed, Cecilia had not known. It had been a sudden freak on the part of Stairs to come back and see her once again before leaving for India. "I suppose he was going to stay with the

Lovells. You know they live at the far side of Burnley."

"Yes; I know. It seems very likely. I hope," his mind going back to Cecilia and Gaveston, "they will arrive in time."

"Oh! I hope so. Oh, poor, poor Cissy! Of course," hastily, "she knew him much longer than I did—much more intimately. She would naturally feel it more. You can see that."

"Of course," says Wortley, who is growing desperate beneath the knowledge that the baldness of his replies must seem suspicious to her; but the more he racks his brains for ordinary sympathetic expressions, the less he finds to say.

"Her face was so white—so changed!" says Nell miserably. "Oh, if only I could have gone with her. But I could be of no use to her—none at all; chained here as I am —a mere log—a burden."

She breaks again into bitter sobs, wild now and heart-rending.

"Oh, I must speak to you—I must," cries she. "Stephen, what is the good of your standing over there pretending you know nothing about it when—— Oh, my poor Cissy, it will kill her. And Peter . . . Oh! *what* is to be done?"

Wortley has come back to her.

"Let us think it over. Let us *see* what can be done," says he gently. "And try not to cry!" His voice is low and steady and strong, yet full of passionate entreaty. He has drawn a chair close to her, and impulsively, without thinking, he slips his arm under her head, and draws her to him. In the distress of the moment he fails to know surprise at the fact that he has had the courage to do this, and at the still greater wonder that she does not repulse him. Nay, more, she seems grateful for the tender support, turning her face to him, and hiding it against his arm, as if she finds comfort in his kindly touch. After a few minutes, indeed, her sobs grow less.

"What frightens me most," she goes on presently, "is what Peter will think about it. He never knew that Cissy loved . . Philip Stairs. And, indeed, it was all over. Oh, yes, quite all over. She had become reconciled. . . . And Peter knew nothing. He was happy with her. And now this awful thing has happened, breaking down the silence of years . . . betraying the whole sad story. How—*how* will it be with them after this?"

Wortley makes no answer. He has at last waked to the stupendous fact that Nell is lying with her dainty head upon his arm, contented—comforted. It seems too great a thing for belief! And yet there can be no doubt about it. The lovely face, now pale and distressed by tears, is beneath his eyes. A little ringlet of her hair is lying on his sleeve. And all too late, too late!

The poignancy of this thought—the terrible grief that lies in it, kills, in a measure, his sympathy with her grief. He hardly hears her, indeed, so lost is he in bitter dreaming on what might have been.

"If only I could have gone with them," says Nell, "I might have done something, or perhaps said something, to smooth matters. I might have softened the truth to Peter. I might have helped Cissy to some self-control. Oh!" with a shudder, "it is fearful to be tied like this. Here—here I lie, worse—far worse than dead."

The light from the distant lamps falling on her face makes it look even paler than it is. Death seems near her at this moment.

"Don't say that," exclaims he sharply. "Besides, you know Sir Jefferson gave hope. He spoke of time."

"Ah! words. Words!"

She sighs heavily.

"Why not," eagerly, "let yourself hope?"

"That," reproachfully, "is cruel advice."

"No. No. There must be grounds for it. See now, of late you have been looking stronger—more cheerful. To-night," with another rapid, fearful glance at her face, that is so dreadfully white and worn. "Of course to-night you are not yourself, but yesterday and all last week I have noticed a great change in you, and all for the better. Come now, take heart; you *are* stronger?" It is a question. She hesitates about answering it, and then almost irritably:

"I am afraid so!"

"Afraid! Nell!"

"Don't you see? Don't you understand? I am better, but I shall never be well. I shall never walk again. I know that. I shall live and live, and live, and always *here*," with a shuddering glance at the cushions. "Feeling better means so many more months, perhaps years, of it. Oh, no," with a sharp indrawing of her breath. "Not years, I hope. I have had enough of it. Sometimes," turning her sad eyes to his, "it has occurred to me that when I am dead, I shall lie here still. There will be so little difference. I shall be only a little stiller—a little whiter, that is all."

A groan escapes him.

"Can't you think of something else?"

"I can't. It is all I have to think of. Though, sometimes, I have other fancies . . . that some one is coming in through that door there to measure me for my coffin. No," quickly. "Don't let that distress you. Those are some of my happiest moments. I used to think"—mournfully—"that I should hate to die. The thought of death was horrible to me, but now—now I am afraid I shall live!"

Here the poor child, overcome with grief, both for herself and for Cecilia, hides her face against his sleeve again, and cries bitterly.

"Those who love me should pray for my death!" says she.

"I shall never pray for that," says Wortley. "And—I love you!"

There is a short silence. She stirs restlessly, and presently moves her head from his arm back to the cushions again. Wortley, pushing away his chair, rises to his feet.

"You are very kind. And I know you wish to comfort me," says she. "But—you go too far. To love me—*me*. You have forgotten, I think . . . ."

"I have remembered!" says he. "Well or ill, living or dead, I shall love you, and you only!"

He turns abruptly, to walk up and down the room with rapid strides, descriptive of his state of mind. Presently he stops close to her again.

"All this is madness," exclaims he, almost violently. "You ought to be taken abroad. Change of air, of scene would cure these morbid thoughts. In France or Italy you would grow better, and——"

"Better—better," petulantly. "I don't want to grow better. I want to be *well*. I want to run about as I used to do, to drive— to ride." Her face changes. "Oh, no"— with a quick, most unexpected gasp of terror —"I never want to *ride* again." She had raised her head a little in her excitement, but now falls back again, with a dull laugh—a laugh more sad than tears. "I need not have been so frightened, need I? I shall never be able to——" She breaks off once more, now thoroughly unnerved. "Oh," cries she bitterly, "never—never again. I shall never do anything again. My life is done— finished. And so soon. Oh!"—turning to him with frightened, anguished eyes—"it is *too* soon!"

"It is, God knows!" says he. He falls on

his knees beside her, smitten to the very core of his heart. It is all so inexpresssibly sad—so hopeless—so forlorn. She is trembling, cowering before her cruel fate, with both her little shaking hands pressed against her eyes.

"Try to bear it," says he, feeling what a mockery his words are. Try? She will *have* to bear it, whether she likes it or not! Taking the hand nearest to him, he holds it in a firm pressure, and stooping, presses his lips to the back of it.

Perhaps this kiss, coming as it does from his grief and the disquietude of his soul, touches her. She makes no attempt at the moment at all events to withdraw her hand—she appeals to him in another way.

"Would you"—her voice is very quiet—"lift my pillow a little?"

It is a tacit command to him to release the hand, and instantly he lets it go. Raising her lightly—as he has so often done since her accident—he re-arranges the pillows, and lays her back again upon them tenderly.

In the lifting of her, however, it has seemed

to him (a mere fond hope perhaps) that she is more able to help herself than formerly. She had put her elbow down upon the edge of the sofa, for example, and with the aid of it had almost raised herself without any assistance of his. A month—three weeks ago, she could not have done that. Surely it is a good sign—the best sign of all— that health and strength are returning to her—that the injury to her back may not be so altogether hopeless as they have imagined.

"You ought to see Sir Jefferson again," says he abruptly.

"No. No more false hopes," says she, smiling at him a little sadly.

"But supposing they were not false?"

She makes a gesture, as if pushing something aside. The false hope, perhaps—and he feels it would be useless to argue with her now, after these long hours of strain. Now the little clock on the mantelpiece chimes eight.

"So late!" says she, rather faintly. "And you have had no dinner, and there is still a long ride before you. Oh! I am so sorry. How selfish of me to keep you. Your dinner will be quite spoiled by this time."

"And the cook furious," says he, piling up the agony. He laughs gaily. "Do you know I had forgotten all about it, but now that you remind me of it, I am starving. And you—where is your dinner? You were not the only selfish one, you see. I forgot all about yours. Let me ring the bell, and order you something."

"Oh! as for me, I can have something at any moment. But you——And to tell you the truth, I am not hungry."

"That's nonsense," says Wortley. "Every right-minded person is hungry at eight o'clock. I am, for one. See here. I'll make a compact with you. If you will promise to eat your dinner, I'll promise to stay and eat it with you. It will be basely inhospitable to say No to that, as I shall certainly get no dinner, or, at all events, a most uncomfortable one, if I go home now."

This naturally settles it. Women, as a rule, are not inhospitable, and it goes to Nell's heart to think of his being hungry here in her own house—as it is for the moment.

"Ring the bell," says she promptly, an order obeyed with alacrity by him, and which brings Marshall on the spot in a minute or two.

"Will you bring me some dinner here, Marshall?" says Nell. "And——" She hesitates.

"And will you bring *me* some too, Marshall?" puts in Sir Stephen, coming boldly to his own rescue, as much as Nell's. "And will you tell the cook, that I should take it as a favour if she would for once try to regard me as two persons instead of one?"

Marshall has gone away, discreetly smiling, only to presently re-appear again, headed by old Jenkins, the butler, who bustles in full of importance—with a dignified air, and a tray most excellently loaded.

And now a little table is drawn close to Nell's couch, and the tray is laid upon it, with its chicken, delicately roasted, and some finely-sliced ham, and a very special little salad, and some other necessaries, and at Sir

Stephen's elbow another little table to be looked at after, with a jelly and a small bottle of champagne, and biscuits and some curaçao.

It is quite a pleasant little dinner in spite of everything, and there can be no doubt but that Nell is very much the better for it. Had he not been there to persuade her to eat—to coax her to have a little bit of chicken, a mere suspicion of jelly, half a wine-glass of champagne—she would unquestionably have gone to bed without anything, or that poor substitute for something, upon which so many women fall back in hours of grief—a cup of tea. But in her anxiety to make him eat, she had eaten too, and is now feeling stronger and more hopeful. However, thinking of him and the good dinner he had missed at home, she grows remorseful.

"You have had a wretched dinner," says she regretfully.

"I have had the best dinner I ever had in my life," returns he, " and undoubtedly the most enjoyable one. I also consider I have won a victory. I have made you do something against your will. You have eaten something too."

Nell reflects on this. Certainly, he *has* finished the chicken and the ham, and there is only as much jelly left as one could swear by. Perhaps he has not been so badly treated after all.

"I think you must go now," says she gently.

"I suppose I must. Can't I do anything for you before I go? You—the others being away—is there nothing I can do?"

"Nothing, thank you," flushing faintly. "Marshall can do all I want." She holds out her hand to him, and taking it, he looks at her with a penetrating glance.

"You will not think too much? You will try to be hopeful, and to sleep?"

"Yes. Yes." She smiles up at him. He hesitates a moment, then stooping, presses for the second time a kiss upon her hand and goes.

* * * * *

The storm has risen and is now howling madly—dashing showers of rain falling between the gusts of wind, but through the ride homewards her vision travels with him. Nell, as he found her crying—and then Nell with her head upon his arm: after which comes the memory of the little friendly intimate dinner, that tiny impromptu meal that could hardly go by so dignified a name. He had been allowed to help her, to tend on her, to tell her that this was good for her, or that. They had dined together. They two, alone! Oh! if only all had gone well with her, they two might have dined together all their lives, he always tending, caring for her—her servant—her slave.

CHAPTER XVI.

"Alas! for sorrow is all the end of this!"

THE storm is still rising, and now blinding, violent showers of rain are dashing along the darkened roadways—making more full, the already swollen rivulets that run by the edges of them — and clattering like hail against the windows of the carriage! The noise of their angry battery seems to make more deadly the silence of the occupants of it.

Not a word had been said by either of them since leaving Gaveston Park. What word indeed was there to be said? All the naked, miserable, unexpected (and therefore thrice hideous) truth, had been told, and to waste further words over it seemed obviously impossible. To thresh it out, to reduce it to a still greater state of nudity—what good could come of that?

Yet the silence was ghastly. The more so,

in that both, in an unconscious way felt nothing could break it. Cecilia, lying back in her corner of the carriage deaf and blind to everything save the question—" Is it life or death that lies before me at the end of my drive?"—could not have spoken had she tried, and Gaveston would not.

Every now and then a flash of lightning lit up the country side, showing it bare, storm-swept, desolate. Sometimes the flashes illuminated the inside of the carriage, showing no less a storm in there, and no whit less of desolation. Both faces were set, as if turned into stone, but there was misery (if of a different quality) in the eyes of each.

Once, when the carriage in the natural darkness that usually follows upon the supernatural brilliance of a lightning flash, was driven over a huge stone threatening to overturn it, Cecilia threw out her hand, and a sharp cry escaped her. But Gaveston felt that there was no fear for herself in that quick cry, only a dread lest anything should occur—any accident—to prevent her being in time to see her lover alive.

His lips grew compressed as that word "lover" came to him, and an almost brutal expression replaced the usual gentle serenity of his face.

At last some stray lights from hamlets on the way side, coming quicker and quicker, one after the other, warn them that they are nearing their destination—on the outskirts of the little town of Burnley. And presently taller houses loom through the darkness and the sound of the horses' feet grows less loud, as the noise of humanity grows louder. A gas lamp here and there, stationed like sentinels along the road, far apart, but evidently with an eye on each other and all that pass them by, bespeaks the town, and then, quite unexpectedly as it were, they have entered it, and presently the horses draw up before the principal hotel of this little place—an hotel that might without prejudice have been called an inn, except that it lacks the roses and honeysuckles, and sanded parlours and general cleanliness, that are usually connected with that wayside place of rest. Here, there are no roses or honeysuckles—it would naturally be madness to expect them at this time of year. But alas, the sanded parlours are not here either, and as for the cleanliness—the least said the better. Altogether it is a squalid, hideous hole.

The door is open, and the little hall inside —grimy, as though a scrubbing brush has not seen it for a twelvemonth—is low, and dull, and mean in the extreme. It goes to Cecilia's heart that *he* should be here. Here! in such a place. And—perhaps—*dying* here. Oh, no—no—no!

A waiter has come forward. A bowing, obsequious person, whose face is as grimy as the hall, and who would have been considerably the better for a change of linen and an energetic bath.

"You have a gentleman staying here," says Gaveston abruptly. His tone is low, but there is not the faintest suspicion of feeling in it. "Captain Stairs!"

"Yessir."

Here Cecilia, with one step, is at the waiter's side.

"He?" stammers she.

"Yes. Captain Stairs, M'."

"He——" her lips almost refuse to move, "He—" forcing the words through her teeth, "is alive?"

"Yes, 'm," sympathetically, "jest that." Perhaps she is a wife, or a sister. "But——"

Cecilia sways a little and Gaveston catches her arm. His touch restores her. He is not aware of it, but it hurts her.

"This lady wishes to have a sitting-room for a few minutes," says Gaveston, without glancing at Cecilia, however. Feeling her stronger, he has taken away his hand from her arm, quickly—with undeniable haste—as Cecilia through all, is aware.

"Well, sir," says the waiter, pointing in a somewhat embarrassed fashion to the little dining-room, "the salone is vacant at present." His tone is extremely apologetic, and as he speaks, he throws open the door of the "salone" on his left with not altogether the air to which he has accustomed himself.

"You had better go in there," says

Gaveston. His voice is low, and clear, and level, and by no means dictatorial in any way—yet Cecilia draws back.

"I want to go to him," says she, *her* voice is low too, but it is piercing. "I," she looks full at her husband defiantly, miserably, "have come to see him."

"And I have brought you here to see him," returns he coldly. "In the meantime, if you can control your impatience, there are a few things to be seen to"—he pauses—"It is cold out here. You had better go in—for a few minutes."

And indeed the hall *is* cold. The boisterous wind outside is blowing fiercely through the imperfectly-fastened door, and the loose casements of the windows. The waiter is still standing with the handle of the open door in his grasp, and Cecilia gliding past him, stands within the room—a faded, melancholy apartment, dirty, uninteresting, and unpleasantly redolent of food, and smoke. It is warm, however—a bright fire sparkling in a grate, that would have been big enough to satisfy the chills of a room three times its size.

Cecilia out of sight, Gaveston turns to the waiter. There cannot be said to be undue haste in his manner, but the waiter tells himself the "gent" wants to know all he can know, in a hurry. Waiters are wonderful!

"Who is with him?" asks he.

"The doctor, sir."

"Go and tell the doctor that some friends of Captain Stairs have arrived, and wish to see him."

"Yessir."

The man had obeyed him, and is now, indeed, up three steps of the stairs, when Gaveston checks him. Peter has turned to do this, and has therefore his back to the "*salone.*"

"Will he live?" asks he.

"No, sir. No, I'm told!"

"Well, give "——" my message to the doctor," he was going to say, but the rush of a slender body past him, the swift flying of small feet up the staircase near him, killed the words upon his lips.

Cecilia is now half-way up the stairs—and *now* she has turned a corner, and is out of sight. Mr. Gaveston looks after her, his face quite expressionless, and yet it seems in some queer way to have grown older, sterner.

"Pore lady! O' course she's hanxious," says the waiter, with the compassion that all waiters seem to have in a high degree—laid by in tons, as it were—for use as occasion offers, and ready to be turned on at a moment's notice. "The gen'l'man's wife, p'raps, sir?"

"No, my wife," says Peter Gaveston in a singularly clear tone. "Mrs. Gaveston of The Park."

"Yessir."

Gaveston's tone is so devoid of all feeling, that the waiter misses the point he was so very close to, a minute ago. No romance here evidently. The captain must be the lady's brother.

"How did it happen?" asks Peter slowly.

"Well, sir, it was"—the waiter lowers his voice, and shakes his head in true confidential style, "the most extraordinary thing you ever 'eard of. 'E was steppin' out of the train 'ere, at our station—seems he was comin' to stay with some people round about us"—the waiter is plainly of the opinion that the whole neighbourhood, aristocratic and otherwise, to say nothing of the town, belongs to the proprietors of the "Royal Hotel"—as it is most inappropriately called. "I forget the name just now, but"—catching his lips in his fingers and pulling them out, as if by their help to bring his brain to a happy state of remembrance.

Peter's hands clench involuntarily, but his face remains set, unreadable.

"Major Lovell, perhaps," says he. As he makes this suggestion for the waiter's future guidance, a sense of loathing fills him.

"I dessay, sir, very likely. The Major, one way or another, is always 'aving guests, keeps a open 'ouse, 'e does."

"How did it happen?" asks Sir Peter.

"Well, sir, as 'e stepped out o' the train, there was a luggage barrow coming along, and—there had been rain off and on, sir, as you may remember, and it appears the platform was greasy, and the barrow was 'eavily loaded and ran against 'im, and tripped 'im up, and 'e fell with his forehead crash against a trunk that was iron bound at the edges, and, Law, sir, ain't it easy to kill some folk, and damn 'ard to kill the others?—begging your parding, sir, I'm sure."

The waiter had a mother-in-law.

" You mean to say——"

" That was all, sir. They picked 'im up and brought 'im 'ere, and Doctor Durrant 'e says as 'ow there isn't a chance for 'im—won't live till morning, he says. Seems he was delicate, 'ad bin abroad, and——but I beg parding, sir, o' course you know all that, being a friend o' his."

Peter is silent. To let that word " friend " go by without contradiction, is almost more than he can bear. But the child! The mother of his child must be protected.

" Is he sensible ? " asks he presently.

" Now and again, sir, but not for the past hour, I'm told. 'E was sensible in the afternoon, and sent a telegram, I'm told, to some people 'e knew." Here the waiter pauses, and casts an inquisitive glance at the tall, immovable gentleman, whose eyes are always so persistently bent upon the soiled tarpaulin at his feet.

" Yes, I saw it."

It is the nearest approach to a lie that Peter had ever told in his life, or at all events since manhood forced the meaning of honour, and right, and wrong upon him. " I think I shall go up now," says he, after a moment's painful thought.

" Yessir."

The waiter prepares to lead the way, but Peter motions him to one side.

" I can go alone," says he, coldly ; he knows he is dreading what the waiter might see, if he opened the door of the sick chamber for him. He puts the man to one side with an air of authority, and goes slowly up the stairs.

" Yessir, right 'and, sir, first door," says the waiter, loquacious to the last.

CHAPTER XVII.

> " Pain smote her sudden in the brows and side,
> Strained her lids open, and made burn her eyes;
> For the pure sharpness of her miseries,
> She had no heart's pain, but mere body's rack.
> But at the last her beaten blood drew back
> Slowly upon her face, and her stunned brows
> Suddenly grown aware and piteous,
> Gathered themselves."

THE room is very dim, only one small lamp burning at the far end of it. This casts a dull shadow on the dingy bed where lies the dying man. Within the grate a sickly fire is flickering—going out for want of tendance, as though they had forgotten to poke it, or thought it needless to keep it up—and all through the room the nauseous odours of restoratives and other medicines are floating.

Gaveston, with one hurried glance at the bed, takes in all the details, then turns determinedly away. He knows that Cecilia is kneeling beside it, the hand of the unconscious man clasped in both her own, and with her face pressed against it. There is unutterable misery in the attitude, a silent agony of despair, and he marks that too and remembers it—for ever! The slender, dainty figure, crouching in its silken draperies, and costly furs—so intolerably out of keeping with their hideous surroundings—the small, proud head so prone, the utter *abandon* of the whole picture, burns itself into his memory, and stays with him always.

At the end of the room, near the dim lamp, an old man—a very old man—the doctor evidently—and a woman are conversing in low tones. Gaveston goes straight to them, and the doctor looking up, makes a gesture of commiseration.

"I regret, sir," says he, in the quavering tones of old age, but with much kindliness, "that I have no good news to give you!"

"Is there no hope?" Gaveston's voice being necessarily lowered, the harshness and want of sympathy in it is unheard by the two listeners.

"None, sir. None. If you would like to telegraph——"

"To telegraph?"

"For another doctor; but I may as well tell you honestly that it would be of no use. An hour or two—perhaps minutes—must bring the fatal close to this sad tragedy."

"I shall not telegraph," says Gaveston—his voice is still so low as to be meaningless to the listeners, and the lamplight is too uncertain to let the old Doctor's eyes read the expression on his face. The nurse has withdrawn a little distance.

"This lady," says Gaveston presently, indicating the motionless kneeling figure by the bedside—she——" he stops short, "could we be left alone for a little while?"

"Certainly, sir," says the old man courteously. He bows. "These family afflictions are very terrible," he goes on softly in all good faith, and Gaveston does not undeceive him. Everyone will know to-morrow, of course, but in the meantime——" And it is the more grievous here, in that nothing can be done. There is only *one* thing to be done, sir, and that is to throw one's grief upon our God!" Gaveston could have laughed aloud. "I shall take care you are not interrupted until you want me, or until"—solemnly—"the end."

He mumbles something to the nurse, who very thankfully follows him out of the room and downstairs, with a view to getting a cup of tea, and having a gossip with the landlady, who is a cousin of hers. In Burnley, as in all small places, everybody is first or thirty-first cousin to everybody else.

A small room opening off the chamber of death, Gaveston goes slowly into it, the darkness—the loneliness being a source of strange comfort to him. Always the picture of the slight figure lying crushed against the side of the bed is before him, and here in the darkness, with nothing to come between him and his mental vision of it, it stands out boldly, and can be viewed by him as plainly as though he were in its bodily presence.

He had heard with a savage satisfaction that Stairs was dying, the traitor who had partaken of his hospitality, and then betrayed him—who, under shelter of his roof, had stolen from him his most cherished possession, leaving his house desolate unto him henceforth. All Stairs' qualms of conscience, all his strivings after honour, are, of course, unknown to him, and only the perfidy stands out clear and distinct.

Of what is *she* thinking now, he asks himself, in this dark room—a room so cold, that but for his burning thoughts, he would have felt frozen. *Her* perfidy had been no whit less than his. The woman who, calling herself his wife, had deliberately day by day deceived him with false words and smiles— her heart all the time throbbing for another. Of what is she thinking now?

*   *   *   *   *

God alone could give an answer to that question. Cecilia herself, kneeling, heartbroken, with her lips pressed to the nerveless hand beneath them, could not. She hardly knows how it is with her. A numbness of spirit, a deadly quiet has followed on her passionate expectancy. Her senses seem dulled, her heart a void.

Presently she stirs, and raising her eyes, looks long with trembling eagerness in the still face before her. How calm, how still. Already the earthly look has left it, and the sweet strange sternness of death is lying on lip and brow.

"Phil!" whispers she softly, as one might to a sleeping child that has slept so long that one fears it will never wake again. "Phil!" —Slowly she creeps to her feet, and bends down over him, and slowly too, and with indescribable tenderness—draws her hand across his forehead, and through the dark masses of his beautiful hair.

"Phil!" breathes she again for the third time — it is an appeal so anguished — so fraught with an intense and overwhelming desire to bring him back again, if only for a moment—to see him eye to eye, to hear him, if possible— to let him know she had come at his call—*so* full it is of all these wild and desperate longings, that though the voice is but a whisper, it seems to reach him, to touch the heart now nearly cold, that has beat for her, and her only, all his life.

Whether the voice really reached his dying senses, or whether in the throes of death a last wave flung him once again for a moment upon the strand of life, no one can say—but at this moment he stirs a little, and opens his eyes full upon her. In that supreme moment he sees and knows her; a faint—a mere shadow of a smile sweeps across his lips—a heavy sigh breaks from them; and then the slight flicker of recognition in them dies away, and the eyes, still open, stare—with the awful stare of death, not *at* her, but *through* her, into the immeasurable beyond.

> " The colour of fair red
> Was gone out of his face, and his blood's beat
> Fell, and stark death made sharp his upward feet
> And pointed hands; and without moan he died."

He is dead indeed. But Cecilia will not believe it. Her hand is still upon his head, and still the heat is in him—but presently — presently those awful eyes, immutable, calm, dreadful, appeal to her, and with a wild, strangled cry, she draws back her hand slowly, and slowly too, raises it to her own.

The low, despairing cry reaches Gaveston in his dark room, and brings him to the one outside, where the dim flicker of the now fading lamp seems only to make darkness visible. Through the gloom he can see Cecilia, her hand crushed against her forehead, her body thrown back. Her eyes are wild. As he approaches her, she turns.

"He is dead!" says she, and then again—"Dead!"—as if surprised at the word—as if not believing. Gaveston, bending over the bed, looks at the dead man lying there, and then back again at her. The awful misery in her eyes touches him through all the hard coverings that grief and rage and scorn have laid upon his heart.

"Men," says Ruskin, "are for ever vulgar precisely in proportion as they are incapable of sympathy."

Sympathy wakes in Peter's breast—but it is the bare, far-off sympathy he would have felt for any other human suffering thing, and does not appeal to him as being a sentiment felt by him specially for her.

"It is all over," says he, gently—it is an icy gentleness, however. "You had better go home."

"Home?" She looks at him as if not understanding.

"To Gaveston Park, then," says he coldly.

She makes a movement as if to go back to her dead, and he moves aside as if to give her perfect facility for the step. This stops her, she looks at him, and then at the pale face on the pillow, and there her sad gaze remains.

"I shall see to all necessary arrangements," says Gaveston, interpreting her glance rightly. His tone is stiff and hard, but Gaveston's word is a word not to be doubted at any time or under any circumstances. "To-morrow—I shall see—I shall give orders. In the meantime you will do no good by staying here."

"But to leave him—*alone!*"

She is trembling, shivering. She goes back hurriedly to the miserable bed, where the dead man is lying with fixed, faded eyes staring always before him.

"Your son is alone too!" says Gaveston, in a loud, strange tone. "That man is dead —your son is alive! You sacrificed him when the man was living, will you"— violently—"sacrifice him still, even when the man is dead?"

But Cecilia can see nothing but the beloved face, the hand lying upon the quilt, as when last she held it—the silent, sightless eyes. She falls again upon her knees, and again her head sinks upon the hand that already is growing cold and stiff.

"Oh! my God!" says Gaveston.

The cry bursts from him, and something in it pierces to her soul. It has reached her, though, when all his other entreaties have failed. Trembling still, she rises to her feet, lays the dead hand carefully against the dead side, and with one last long look, bids her loved dead, farewell for ever.

"I will go home," says she.

* * * * *

The storm is still raging on their homeward drive. The heavens are alight with constant flashes, and the horses, startled and unnerved, swerve violently now and then from one side of the road to the other. In between are crashing showers of rain, and an Egyptian darkness—

> "And now the heaven is dark, and bright, and loud,
> With wind, and starry drift, and moon and cloud,"

and then again the darkness, and the violent rain, and lightning!

Gaveston's soul is full of bitterness. All bad things come back to him, making this black hour still blacker, and rendering him a prey to misery. Little things—absurd, insignificant at birth—now seem to grow to a huge height, and kill all softer memories behind! That day, for instance, that Mrs. Chance told him that she—(Cecilia is still "she" to him—our best-beloved, as well as our best-hated, are always very personal pronouns to us)—thought him ugly, comes back to him now, standing out clearly from quite a mass of much more important matter, with a singular distinctness. He had thought nothing of it then—he had indeed, laughed at it as one of Cecilia's funny ways, but now———

Crash goes a clap of thunder, breaking off his thoughts for a moment. A moment only. Now they roll on again, swiftly as ever. What is it that Shakespeare says about women? "Soft, mild, pitiful and flexible." Ay! she had been soft and mild enough, and flexible too, but pitiful—— No. There is no pity in her—for him, at least, or for her child, or———

A sharp sound of weeping—a violent, terrible outburst of grief comes to him from the opposite side of the carriage. It is as short as sharp. It was as the cry of a bird shot on the wing, and ceases as suddenly. Gaveston listens to it, waiting for a repetition of it—but no repetition comes. Having listened long enough to assure himself that there is no more to hear, he leans back again in his corner, with his back to the horses (he could not have sat next her), his thoughts having gained a keener edge from that strange outburst. What did it mean, that paroxysm of grief? What could it mean but confirmation strong of all that has gone before?

> " No hinge, nor loop,
> To hang a doubt on."

And now they are at the Park gates, and now pulling up before the hall-door.

Gaveston leans forward.

"Try to collect yourself," says he. He tells himself always that their little son's interests are before him, not hers, or his.

"Oh! dear Heaven!" says she. It is a mere whisper, but full of all the weariness of this weary world. She rises, pulling her furs round her face as if to protect her from the vulgar gaze.

"You had better go to your room at once," says he, as he helps her to alight. Even in his scorn of her, he considers her comfort.

She moves past him, up the stairs, and into the corridor. Beyond her a light is streaming through the doorway. It is Nell's room, and as her light footfalls reach it, Nell's voice cries eagerly :

"Cissy—is that you, Cissy?"

But Cecilia, dead at heart, goes on, refusing to hear her, though Heaven alone knows what hours of anguish had gone by to make up the sum of that frightened, eager cry.

"Cissy—Cissy!"

Again the poor child, chained to her bed, calls aloud—now bitterly—hearing the steps go by, and Cecilia, pausing, listens—and as the misery of it becomes clear to her, through all her own misery, she turns back.

"You have come, darling," says Nell, holding out little, fragile arms to her. "Come here, Cissy! Come here to me. You will kiss me *now!*"

Cecilia leans over her, but to kiss her brings her somehow to her knees, and this attitude reminds her cruelly of that last sad scene.

"He is dead!" says she.

"Dead! Oh! poor, *poor* Phil!"

Not a word of admonition, or censure, or pity for herself! Only pity—pity pure and heartfelt, and most divine, for Phil. Cecilia, whose heart is feeling like a stone, creeps into the little sister's arms, and cries, and cries, as she has never cried before, and so her wounds find ease. And soon, sweet words persuade her, to "undress here, and steal in beside me," and with Nell's tender arms around her, she sleeps at last.

CHAPTER XVIII.

"In many a stead Doom dwelleth, nor sleepeth day nor night."

TIME, after this, for many weeks went but indifferently for the people at the Park. Gaveston rode, drove, sat on the Bench, and in his seat in church on Sundays as usual, but with a face changed almost beyond recognition. It seemed as if everything was outside and beyond him, far away as it were, and as though he had no real connection with them. To his wife he was courtesy itself, but he never spoke to her unless compelled to do so, and he purposely avoided her society. He told himself she had ceased to be anything to him, that he no longer felt either love or hatred for her, and day by day this feeling grew. She could live in his house, and sit at the head of his table, but that was all. A great gulf yawned and separated her from him.

For all this Cecilia, at first, was sincerely grateful. To be forgotten, to be ignored by the man she had so wronged was what she most desired. To dwell upon her grief—to give herself up to it was all the comfort left to her. Again and ever again that scene by the dying man's bed came back to her, and again she knelt and pressed her cold lips upon the hand that was even colder. One trouble she had—a trouble so many know—and that was the difficulty of recalling the face of her dead. Hour after hour she would sit trying to think of Philip as he had been in life—as he had been in death—but always the face escaped her. It would not come back, and tormented by the longing to see him—even with her inward sight—she would pace her room backwards and forwards, with straining eyes, and hands tightly clasped.

But after a while this fever died away, and one day all at once she saw him quite clearly as he had been when living, and soothed by this consummation of her desire, she grew gradually calmer, and when many weeks had flown, the pain grew easier to bear. And it was then, perhaps, that, having been loved and tended with such jealous care and affection all her married days, she began to feel the loss of the great love, that once had hedged her round.

She faded as the days went by, growing paler and more silent, and presently a sort of indifference took her—and she forgot her beauty even—and to clothe herself in those pretty garments that used to be her delight in earlier, lighter days.

And this vexed Gaveston, though he would not confess it, for what was she to him now? Mere

" Dust and ashes once found fair to see."

Sometimes he told himself that if she had come to him then, when the man was dead, and flung herself upon his compassion, and told him all, he might have forgiven her. But he misjudged himself there. He would *not* have forgiven—he would have thrust her back, repulsing her, loathing the confidence — yet he had persuaded himself that she should have spoken! It was her part. Her silence hardened him, rendering him the more suspicious. Why did she not speak? Was it fear that prevented her?

And this went on for many days; the artificial existence they were leading, telling upon them more morally perhaps than physically. "But as the days change, men change too," and presently there fell that into their lives that roused them to a further sense of being; though it laid one of them very low, even at death's door.

But before that came, Gaveston had found comfort of a sort. The child was always there with his pretty prattle and his happy ways, and the child was not to be repulsed, or set aside or ignored in any way. There was comfort in the small glad creature; and during the morning ride across the free, open common, with the boy beside him on his pony and the wild sea breeze tearing across their faces, and mingling with the merry laughter of the child, the desire of life came back to Gaveston—the love for the child falling like dew upon his crushed and wounded heart.

But for the child's mother there was no softening, no forgiveness—only, a continuing and increasing wrath.

He put her deliberately from him, refusing to let himself dwell upon her. He gave her no place indeed in his thoughts, and if by chance he was compelled to think of her, as when he wondered at her new lack of daintiness in her frocks, or her obstinacy in refusing to say one word to him of her dead lover, he hurried over the thought as one does over matters hateful.

* * * * *

And now the world is uplifting itself once more, casting off its late sad trammels. There is an odour of newly-turned earth in the air, and the sweet winds, crisp and strong, are carrying news of a fresh birth to everything. Little twitterings come from beneath the branches, and louder twitterings still from the ivy that covers half the sides of the house, and the streams are running merrily down below, and that one must be a *fool*, who does not know that " spring has come up our way."

Here in the woods the little hands—those small, sweet, tiny, childish hands that help the All-Mother—are busy at work, digging and delving here, and picking and pushing there, until at last even her tinier pupils uplift their heads and stare out vaguely upon a fresh world. The baby fronds of the ferns, the delicate green blades of grass, the bursting buds upon the trees, all cry aloud to-day that spring—that *spring* has come.

Touches of the dead king winter are lying all around; but no one thinks of him now, or dreads him. The clear skies, the happy rushing winds speak only of hopes to come, and even where his foot trod heaviest, flowers are now awakening to the glad light of their god—the sun.

> " Primroses now awake
> 'Neath the ruin of the withered brake
>   From nursing shades;
> The crumpled carpet of the dry leaves brown
>   Avails not to keep down
>   The hyacinth blades.

The hazel hath put forth his tassels ruffed,
The willow's flossy tuft
    Hath slipped him free,
The rose amid her ransacked orange hips
Braggeth the tender tips
    Of bowers to be."

*   *   *   *   *

The spring is here indeed, and something more. Something horrible, a battle between life and death. At first no one took any heed of it. There was just a little cloud lying far away down there upon the horizon—but by degrees that little cloud strengthened and grew until now the whole heaven is obscured by it. And the name of the cloud is Fever—Typhoid Fever!

Gaveston at once volunteered as a recruit in the small army of workers that arose to quell this scourge; and Cecilia of all people was the first to come forward and offer to help the nurses and other benevolent women, who were bent on dragging the lower classes —the pitiful ones of the earth—out of the fangs of death. Gaveston had broken through the silence that now always separated them, in an attempt at remonstrance with her about this; but she put him aside with a little gesture and a glance that dwelt in his memory for long afterwards. He had returned that glance with interest. It was made up entirely of reproach—and when three days later he himself gave in, and lay tossing on his bed (attacked by the fell disease that was destroying hundreds in their midst), that glance of hers still dwelt with him, and in his ravings took quite a prominent part.

For days and days he lay there fighting for his life; the doctor growing graver at every visit, and Cecilia, who would let no nurse divide her duties with her, looking paler daily and daily more hopeless.

CHAPTER XIX.

> "Diseased nature oftentimes breaks forth
> In strange eruptions."

Mrs. Cutforth-Boss, half-an-hour after the news of Peter's illness had been disseminated through the neighbourhood, is standing on the hall-door steps of the Park. The managing mania has once more seized hold of Maria. From the first she had not shrunk from the fever or its consequences, and had indeed been one of Dr. Bland's most useful helpers. She knew no fear, and the fever never touched her.

"It," said Mrs. Wilding, chuckling maliciously, "avoided her, like *everything else.*"

Meeting the doctor on the steps now, she informed him she had come to nurse Peter Gaveston, as she felt sure that that silly young woman, his wife, would be equal to nothing but hysterics, at a juncture like this.

But Dr. Bland, who had begun to form

quite a high idea of Cecilia since the beginning of the fever in the country round, and who had noticed the quick and intelligent way in which she had grasped his meaning occasionally, and the deftness of the pretty, idle-looking fingers, and above all, the sympathy she had shown for even the worst and ugliest cases—made a stand.

No; Mrs. Gaveston was quite equal to the strain. Mrs. Cutforth-Boss herself must have noticed how admirably she had behaved all through this terrible time—especially in the case of those poor Browns.

"But this is different!" said the lady. "Her husband, you know—she will infallibly lose her grip with *him* to nurse, and then *I* shall come in."

"The greater the blow, the greater the strength sometimes," said Dr. Bland. "And, at all events, she wouldn't hear of it for a moment. She has even declined the offices of a nurse, and when I remonstrated with her about it, she said she would have one as a *help* if I insisted on it, but that *she* would be the head. That young lady has been spoiled by good fortune, ma'am," said the doctor, taking a pinch of snuff. He said snuff was better than a pipe—though he smoked freely—and that it kept sicknesses from getting into him. " If she had been brought up in a hard school, she would have been a shining light by now."

Poor Cecilia! *Her* school, though set in silks and laces, had been too hard for one poor human thing.

Maria, however, was not to be entirely baffled. She made up her mind there and then, that if she could not save Peter, she would at all events take home that spoiled boy of Cecilia's and save him. She went in therefore in spite of the doctor, and saw Cecilia, and made her proposition about Geoffrey, and Cecilia gladly accepted the offer, being thankful to get the child out of the way of infection.

So Mrs. Cutforth Boss carried him off in triumph, and only just in time, as Mrs. Wilding drove up on the same errand, even before Maria went away victorious with her prize. It must be confessed that Mrs. Wilding heaved a sigh of relief when she saw her go.

"Fast," some people in Bigley-on-Sea called Mrs. Wilding, and some of the others "vulgar." But the soundness of her heart was proved then. In fear and trembling—considering that she had a little, tiny, most beloved son at home—she had still driven forth to take away a neighbour's child, and bring it into her own house, with a view to saving his life!—a child that would perhaps bring infection with him, coming from a fever-stricken household.

The sigh with which she saw Maria depart with Geoffrey was most genuine, and she said "Thank God" under her breath, with perhaps a more prayerful feeling than she had ever known in her life before. Still she *would* have taken Geoffrey home.

Meantime, Mrs. Cutforth-Boss has driven off in triumph, with her prey. Here, now, is a clear case for management!

* * * * *

Before leaving the subject entirely, however, it may be as well—and indeed it is only fair to add—merely as a tribute to Geoffrey's mental strength—that long before his return to the parental roof *he* had most effectually managed Maria! That wonderful woman, who had ridden rough-shod over most of her acquaintances all her life, at last was reduced to abject slavery by one small boy.

When she tried to scold him, he cared nothing for her homilies, only laughed and clutched her round the neck, and kissed her. The child was hungry for kisses in those days, being denied the ones that had been his right from his birth. And when she told him that little boys should be seen and not heard, he laughed too, and threw his toys at her. By degrees he thoroughly demoralised her, and there came at last one awful day when the butler found her running races with him in the garden!

Over this, however, a veil should be drawn. It is, nevertheless, a legend in the Boss family, that once a butler of theirs was discovered on the verge of apoplexy. It was Mr. Cutforth-Boss who discovered him, but Maria indignantly repudiates the idea that *she* had anything to do with it—and, at all events, the butler who recovered, did not betray her. But she was always afraid to dismiss him, so he is there still.

It was dreadful, the lengths to which Geoffrey used to go—even to the invading of Mr. Cutforth-Boss's sanctuary, and the examining of all the awful things therein.

It was a lovely place, he said, and so funny. With the queerest little things in bottles, and crawley-crawlies all over it. Mr. Cutforth-Boss afterwards, poor man, said he was afraid Geoffrey had eaten a good many of them, because only the wings could be found. But Maria cared for none of these things. She drew great stores of culture from the child, and learned from him many things that life up to this had failed to teach her. And from that visit forward, to the end of their friendship, which endured to the close of her life, Maria bowed herself before Cecilia's son.

* * * * *

And all this time Gaveston lay prostrate, whilst above him life and death fought for the mastery.

There had come a time when all seemed over, and when Cecilia who for twenty days had tended him day and night (taking but a little rest now and then) had fallen upon her knees beside his bed, and prayed herself into unconsciousness—then waked to pray again. He had lived through that time, had waked for a moment or two, and had seen and known his wife. She was bending over him at the moment, and his eyes slowly opening, had fixed themselves on hers. There was instant recognition in them, and a weird, terrible, sudden recollection of all that had gone before. It was as the recollection of a drowning man before he goes under for ever. Gaveston had looked straight into his wife's eyes, and two words had passed his lips.

"Too late!" he said.

The doctors decided that he had given himself up, and augured ill from it—but Cecilia knew, and the knowledge burned into her soul! He had meant to tell her that his dying came "too late," that if he had died a year or two ago, Stairs could have *honourably* sought and married her. As he sank back into unconsciousness, she moved away her face as white as ashes.

Even with the shadow of death lying on him, he remembered! She had embittered his life, she was now embittering his death!

After that he rallied a little, causing a slight hope to arise—a vague one, and one they hardly dare to dwell upon—and now to-day the crisis is expected, and the doctors, hanging round his bed, or going backwards on tiptoe, to consult one with the other in the anteroom—now here, now there—make a sort of kaleidoscope to Cecilia, who, on her knees, is watching the pale, emaciated face upon the pillow in its strange sleep of exhaustion, that may mean life—or may mean death.

Downstairs, Nell lying on her couch, is waiting—waiting! Dear Lord! how hard it is to wait, when the limbs are lifeless, and only the heart and head can move. Oh! to be with Cecilia now! to help her, to guard her, to wait with her! She, poor child, fretting on her sofa, feels as though she is going mad in her anxiety to go up there into the silent room—and know.

When he wakes—if ever he wakes again—will he know her—poor, poor Cissy—and forgive her? Surely her devotion during his illness should count for something. And that past madness—has she not suffered for it? How sad she must be now, how frightened.

Suddenly a spasm contracts her face. She —she is frightened too, but there is no one to help her either. Oh! dear—dear Heaven! send some relief—even a servant! Oh! if only she could rise and ring the bell—if she could only hobble so far. . .

Heaven sends her some relief. The door is opened quietly—in the way that people open doors when sickness is in the house, even though the chamber of death be three flights away, and the door that is opened in the basement storey, and Wortley comes in.

He had come over to hear the latest news —to be of some use to the stricken household if possible, but Nell seeing him, feels all at once that speech is beyond her, and after a hurried greeting he goes over to the window to wait there for the end. The poor child's painful anxiety is too pitiful to watch.

Tick, tick, goes the clock on the mantelpiece in a dreadful monotone. It gets on Wortley's nerves at last, and makes him leave the window. He is, indeed, half way across the room, when flying footsteps down the stairs outside can be distinctly heard.

"He is dead!" says Nell.

Her voice sounds dull. She has raised herself on her elbow, and is looking at Wortley with livid lips, but eyes that are brilliant with fear and pain.

"No. No," says he.

The steps are nearer now.

"Oh, God! be *kind* to her!" cries Nell, softly praying.

And now the door is open, and Cecilia stands upon its threshold. She throws up her arms.

"He will live—he will live!" cries she, with a little burst of delirious laughter.

"Thank God!"

The words are on Wortley's lips, but he never utters them. He has turned his glance instinctively on Nell, and there—*there!*——

Great Heavens, she is *standing*—she is tottering forward — her hands outheld to Cecilia!

Wortley rushes to her, and in another moment she lies fainting within his arms.

But she had *stood!* She had made a step forward! To Cecilia, overwrought, this miracle proves too much. She bursts out crying.

CHAPTER XX.

"Lying asleep between the strokes of night,
I saw my love lean over my sad bed."

THE battle of Peter between Life and Death is over. Life has won. And all because of his wife's devotion, attention and care, says old Dr. Bland, whenever he goes on his daily rounds through the neighbourhood.

"Why, my dear sir, we're getting on famously — famously," says he, as he now seats himself beside his patient's bed. "No more fears now. You can defy everybody. How's the pulse, eh?—quite strong, I declare. No use bothering you about it again. 'Pon my word, I think it's your wife wants looking after now, gone to skin and bone, I say, and all through her devotion to you. You'll have to hurry up, my friend, if only to look after *her*. One good turn deserves another, you know!"

The little doctor ambles over to the

window to pull a blind a little to one side, that is letting in the glittering spring sunshine too freely on his patient's face; but Cecilia has forestalled him.

"See now what an admirable nurse," cries the doctor gaily. "Even that little thing did not escape her. Come here, Mrs. Gaveston, and let me tell your husband who it was rescued him from the jaws of death."

"You!" says Cecilia faintly, and in a troubled tone, that all the lightness she tries to throw into it cannot well disguise.

"Who — I? Tut — tut — tut," says the doctor, protruding his lower lip, as he always does when protesting. "I tell you what, Gaveston, the doctor has always less to do with a recovery than the nurse; for the doctor can only give orders, and if the nurse doesn't carry them out, why, where is the patient then? I tell you it all lies in the hands of the nurse," and with a little wave of his hand to Cecilia, who has slunk back amongst the curtains and whose face cannot now be seen, "you must let me congratulate you upon yours."

"I thought there — was — a nurse — from——"

The voice is low and husky, and weak from the bed.

"From Guy's? So there was, but your wife just put her aside. She took the lead, and Mrs. Thompson told me only yesterday that she wished she had served under Mrs. Gaveston in her earliest days, and she would have learned more than she knows now. I daresay," says the doctor laughing, "she was romancing a bit, but honestly, Gaveston, you owe your life, after Heaven, to your wife!"

As he says this he rises, and giving a few fresh instructions for the night to Cecilia, goes his way to carry comfort, or hope, or despair to other houses.

When he has gone, silence falls upon the sick room. Cecilia, still standing half hidden by the bed-curtains, waits patiently for the moment that will tell her Peter has fallen asleep. When quite fifteen minutes have gone by filled with the restless turnings, and the querulous twistings, that belong to the wearied sick, and now the quietness tells her he is again sleeping, she emerges from her hiding-place, and sinking softly, slowly on her knees by the bedside, lays her tired head upon the pillow close to that of the man who has cast her from him, as unworthy.

For a long time she kneels here; first with her eyes upon the silent face, and then—then thoughts crowd round her, and at last her pretty head drops, her lids grow heavy, and . . .

" Why did you do it ? "

The words come to her through a veil, the veil of long wanted sleep, but presently she sits up and thrusts the veil aside, and looks eagerly into the eyes of the man lying upon the pillow.

" Do what ? "

" Bring me back to life."

Cecilia makes no reply. A wave of bitterness passes over her. She lays her head back again upon the pillow near him, and softly, suddenly, without premeditation of any sort, and with a sudden instinct, lays her arm across his throat.

It lies there for a moment, and then he stirs. Feebly—with difficulty—he lifts one hand, as though to push away that other hand from his throat; and, indeed, for a terrible minute she fears that this is his intention, but when his fingers have closed upon her wrist, whatever he may have meant to do at first, he takes no further course, and his fingers remain there.

Presently he moves them up and down her arm, slowly—vaguely.

"You have grown thin?"

"Not so thin as you have."

"Oh! I!" His faint voice is expressive of utter weariness, and through it she knows that he is wishing he were a little thinner still, and at rest, and dead! A feeling of misery too great to be borne sweeps over her. She must give voice to it.

"Peter! may I speak to you?"

"To what end?"

"Silence is killing me! *May* I speak?"

He makes her no answer, and with his head turned from her she cannot read his face, but after a little while, a faint pressure of his fingers on her wrist seems to give her the desired permission.

"I want to tell you—to say to you . . . Peter," desperately, "you must believe me! I—what I have to say is that I never knew how much I cared for you—what a positive necessity you were to me—until I nearly lost you! You," in a stifled tone, "you *must*—you *do* believe me, don't you?"

"Ah! He is dead now!"

"It isn't that!"

"And I should have been dead before you ever met me."

"Peter! Peter!" Perhaps the anguish in her voice reaches his dull senses, that hardly yet have wakened from the sleep that death had so nearly sealed, because now his voice, if fainter, has less bitterness in it.

"You loved him!"

She lets this go by, but he repeats it, the hot feverish hand now burning upon hers in a tightened clutch, that in good health would have been a most masterful hold.

"Yes!" The word is low but clear. How could he have expected another answer?

And if another had been given what could it mean but falsehood, and yet—strange human nature—he resents it. Now the feeble hand *does* try to push her from him, but she, catching hold of the neck of his night-gown, refuses to be thrust aside.

"That is all over," says she quietly—miserably. "And . . . show some pity, Peter. I have no one but you, now."

"Ay! *Now!*" There is a pause, but presently he speaks again. "You have the child."

"I want the child's father too."

Another long silence! She is crying, bitterly, silently—but now some despairing thought comes to her, and she breaks into low, but violent sobbing.

"Peter—*can't* you forgive me?"

Again she waits, and again that feeble hand closes upon hers, with a touch that contains hatred, she tells herself. Ah! this time she will not resist him! He can spurn her now if he will—he may cast her from him . . . He——

Slowly he has taken, and then slowly he lifts the little trembling hand, and as she waits

with beating heart to have it cast back to her
—this poor weak olive branch—he draws it to
him, nearer—nearer—until the palm is lying
on his lips!

Trembling, weeping, she at last dares to
look at him.

He has turned his face to the wall, as if to
hide it away from all men. And from
beneath his closed and sunken lids two slow
tears are stealing down his gaunt cheeks.
But his kiss is still warm upon Cecilia's
palm!

She feels as if her heart is breaking!

Silently the moments fly. She, kneeling
beside his bed, and he with his face averted,
but always with her hand against his lips—
and no word spoken. After a little while she
knows he has fallen asleep—the heavy sleep
of exhaustion, that is so often the sleep of
returning health.

Cecilia, softly releasing her hand, gets up
from her knees and bends over him. There
is a new look upon his face—a look that has
not been there for many a day. There is hope
in it, and a strange sweet peace!

CHAPTER XXI.

"Through thick and thin, both over bank and bush,
In hopes her to attain by hook or crook."

"HERE we are again!" cries Summer, that pretty clown, springing into our midst, almost without a word of warning. The hot, glad sun is glinting upon the full-leaved beeches and all the world seems "afire with roses."

Spring has passed away. Our vestal virgin that "goeth all in white," and now here is June—mad, rampant, laughing all the day, and far into the night, and waking—only to laugh again.

Gaveston's return to life had been a matter of much delight to many people, for Peter in his quiet way had been very universally liked. His wife's devotion to him in his illness had proved a nine days' wonder, and had at once lifted the volatile Cecilia to quite a high position in public opinion—perhaps higher than she even aspired to, or than perhaps she deserved. But what took Bigley-on-Sea by storm, what dwarfed its interest in Peter's recovery, and Cecilia's astonishing wifely devotion, was the fact of Nell's strange recovery.

The big man from town had been brought down again, and had again formed an opinion on Nell's case—a highly favourable one this time, and having pocketed his fee (he was quite as surprised at her miraculous recovery as the least scientific person in Bigley, only he did not say so), had reminded them that he had always said: "Leave it to time. To *time*, Mr. Gaveston!"

Mr. Gaveston nodded, keeping his thoughts to himself. And then the big man had ordered this for Nell—and that — and the other thing, but at all events in spite of him Nell grew stronger daily, and now in this sweet month of June is able to get about again—slowly certainly, and with many halts, and the help of a stick, but always with the next day's performance better than the last.

Mrs. Chance, who is ever on the alert, and as wide awake as an owl at midnight on the prowl for a mouse, had written to Alec from time to time, giving very vague hints of Nell's improvement, until that improvement was sure. And now *very* urgently—seeing that Sir Stephen's visits are still as frequent at The Park, " as when out of his charity " (as Bella insisted on saying) " he went to see that poor crippled girl! "

She had compelled herself to believe this, refusing to acknowledge, even to herself, that Wortley's visits there had a deeper significance.

Last week she wrote again to Grant, desiring him to come at once, and try his fate once more with Nell. And Grant, only too eager to tempt it, had come to-day, and encouraged by many words of Bella's, has walked over to Gaveston Park to find Nell lying in a long chair on the sunny side of the garden. Deep in cushions, and looking lovely if a little fragile still, and with the fresh touch of life's colours on her lips and in her eyes.

Wortley is seated near her, Cecilia hovering round, whilst Gaveston and his little son, at a rustic table, are pouring out the tea.

Just now Cecilia, within the circle of her own family, is popularly supposed to be able to do nothing, but enjoy herself and look lovely. The latter she does to perfection, and for the other, the gay little smile that wreathes her lips at times speaks well for it. A secret—the barest—and besides it is only "the family" that knows a word of it—is afloat, that, later on, before the hard snows fall, Geoffrey's dainty nose will be out of joint. The idea that it may be a little daughter that is to be added to the riches of the house, has taken Nell's fancy by storm, and enthrals her imagination at times. A daughter for Cissy! A son was very good! But a little *girl!*

Grant, crossing the shaven sward to where Nell is lying, is received with great friendliness on all hands. Nell, indeed, seems enchanted to see him; she makes a place for him on her lounge, pulling her skirts aside to give him room, and devotes her whole attention to him. And the young man's heart, seeing her so well, although still so undoubtedly invalided, swells within him.

That Sir Stephen is always beside her,

troubles him at first, but when after awhile Wortley moves away, his heart grows lighter, and he tells himself that Wortley has seen how it is, and is giving him a clear field—that he knows the game is up, and so on.

Here Cecilia brings Nell her tea, and Grant, starting to his feet, hurries across to the little rustic table to bring her some cake.

"No. No," says she, shaking her charming head, with a smile that is as pretty as it can be. And then she lifts herself a little, so as to look over Grant's shoulder, and says to some one beyond—in a clear, distinct tone:

"Stephen! Why don't you bring me my bread and butter?"

Something! What is it? Or was there really anything? Something there must have been, for all at once Grant knows that there is no hope for him—that he has no chance with her—that he is less than nothing to her—and that Wortley is all the world!

As soon as it is possible to him, he rises, and bids her good-bye—if he had a last lingering doubt, the fact that she accepts his going, kindly but indifferently, and never so much as asks him when he is coming again, or how long his leave lasts, or where he will be to-morrow, destroys it.

Cecilia and Gaveston accompany him to the gate, where he parts with them, with a last backward glance towards the garden, that shows him Nell laughing prettily at Wortley —who is, however, looking a little grave and disturbed.

Grant's walk back to his sister's house is filled with thoughts that can scarcely be called pleasant. Those that relate to Bella are, indeed, distinctly unpleasant, and there are moments when he curses himself for his stupidity in being brought to such a pass as this. Bella had distinctly given him to understand that Nell—(*dear* little Nell! for her there is not, even at this heart-broken juncture, a thought that is not altogether loving)—was still free to be wooed and won, and yet half-an-hour in her presence was sufficient to prove to him that her heart was given irrevocably away.

A furious rage against Bella is tearing at his heart as he enters her presence.

"Well?" says she hurriedly. The hope in her tone is evident as she turns to him, but it is extinguished as her eyes meet his.

"*Well?* Nothing is well! I don't know what you meant by telling me what you did this morning."

"Wasn't she glad to see you then?"

"In the sense *you* mean—No!"

"She is a vile coquette then," says Mrs. Chance, with a viperous tightening of her lips.

"She is no such thing," says Grant, almost violently. "And once for all, I may as well tell you that I will hear no word said against her by you, or by anyone."

"You are very complaisant, I must say. You defend her, though she, at the last moment, has thrown you over. Even though you came so many miles to see her, she was not even—as you say—glad to see you?"

"You make a mistake there! She *was* glad to see me. Too glad. Indifferently glad! I should think," says Grant, with a touch of angry reproach, "that anyone with an eye in her head could have seen that she is in love with Wortley."

"She is not!" Bella has changed colour.

"You will tell me next, perhaps, that he is not in love with her?"

"He is *not!*" The same phrase falls from her working lips, but now even more vehemently. "She was ill—he was kind—that is all!"

Grant shrugs his shoulders.

"So much for *your* penetration," says he. He is too much engaged over his own miseries to give heed to the terrible disappointment that is beginning to show itself in her face. "They are as good as engaged in my opinion, if not so already."

"*Your* opinion! What is it worth, I wonder? Engaged! They are *not* engaged. I could almost swear they aren't. Maria would not *hear* of it for one thing."

"Maria does not work this world," says Grant. "And look here. Your saying she is not in love with him, wouldn't hold water for a moment. She"—groaning—"is *that* in love with him, that she can't even eat bread and butter unless he gives it to her."

"Splendid evidence!" says Bella scornfully. "What a fool you are!"

"Evidence enough for me anyway!"

"You ought to wait! To go back. To-morrow she . . ."

"I used to think you a clever sort of girl," says Grant slowly. "You are right, I *am* a fool. No, I shall not go back, and I shall not wait. To stay forlorning round here, is a trifle too much for *me*. And as for to-morrow, I'm off to Ireland by the ten o'clock train."

"So like you," says his sister, her face pale with fear and rage combined. "You haven't the courage to gain your point. I tell you she *doesn't* care for Sir Stephen. And as for him, why, I know he has the *worst* opinion of her——"

"Oh, rot!" says her brother, walking out of the room, and slamming the door behind him.

Even now Bella, who has great staying powers, will not acknowledge to herself that the game is at an end. Maria! Surely Maria will see a way out of this difficulty, if, indeed, difficulty there be. It seems impossible to believe that Stephen is really anxious to marry that ridiculous girl, with her frivolous airs, and a back hopelessly crippled, in spite of what the biggest doctors in Europe may say.

To run upstairs and put on her jacket and her bonnet—she always wears a bonnet as being more decorous, she says—as a fact hats don't become her—and to walk down to Cutforth Hall takes barely half an hour, and Maria being found in the library arranging her husband's books—she always managed her husband's books when *he* refused to be managed, as it took him days afterwards to re‑arrange them — Bella pours out her grievance with eloquent tongue.

"It is impossible, isn't it? You wouldn't hear of it, would you? Just consider! *That* girl of all others. No man's name, or comfort, would be safe with her. Why"—angrily—"don't you *speak*, Maria? You have so often told me that you would not sanction such an engagement, that. . . ."

"I've said a lot of things in my time,"

says Maria, solemnly, flicking the duster to and fro, and occasionally very close to Bella's nose. "And so have you, I daresay. But I have learned to believe, that neither you nor I can prevent Stephen doing just as he likes, either in the way of choosing a wife, or anything else."

"You mean to give in, then?" gasps Bella. "To let him destroy his whole life by marrying this girl. Oh!" She pauses as though too over-filled with righteous indignation to give voice to another syllable. But presently she rallies. "And you——" Her eyes are now flashing with a fire that has something vindictive in it. "*You*, who professed to be a leader of men—to manage the people round you!"

She has turned her glance full on the great Maria, as though expecting and preparing for an explosion from her — but to her surprise it never comes. Mrs. Cutforth-Boss, as though not hearing her, is looking up at the cornice, and drumming her fingers on the table. She is evidently lost in thought. Not unpleasant thought, by any means, judging by the curves of her masculine lips.

"And you really think there is something in it," says she at last. "That Stephen actually means to marry her?" She brings her eyes down from the cornice to look at Bella, and once again hope revives in that intriguer's breast.

"Oh! beyond doubt. Beyond *any* doubt. Alec says it is plain. Unless—unless someone comes forward to prevent Stephen from taking this fatal step, he will undoubtedly marry Miss Prendergast within the year." She looks eagerly at Maria. Surely this is strong enough. *Now* she will come to the rescue. Maria has gone back, however, to her calculations and is again smiling. After a moment she says slowly:

"Nell Prendergast is Geoffrey's aunt! After all then, that boy will belong to me in some sort of a way, before—as you say—the year is out!

Nell's relationship to the child has all at once reconciled her to the marriage. Surely it is children who sway the world!

Bella, with one withering glance at Mrs. Cutforth-Boss, rises to her feet. The game is up.

"Ah! one can see *now*," says she in her softest, most deliberate tones, and with her little hesitation very distinct, but with a glance that is meant to cut the other to the very heart's core, "what a grief it has been to you to have *no children of your own!*" She waits to see the effect of this shot, but Maria can always be depended on when dynamite is about.

She regards Mrs. Chance for a moment with a searching eye and then——

"'Those who live in glass houses—'" quotes she, pointing a bony finger at her—"'should not throw ——' What, going already?"

But Bella vouchsafes no reply—marching out of the room, she closes the door finally behind her. The next day sees her far from Bigley-on-Sea, and I don't know that anyone there has up to this regretted her.

CHAPTER XXII.

> "She also came and heard,
>   O my joy,
> 'What,' said she, 'is this word?
>   'What is thy joy?'
>
> "And I replied, 'O see,
>   O my joy,
> ''Tis thee,' I cried, ''tis thee;
>   Thou art my joy.'"

WORTLEY here in the garden with Nell is feeling sad and depressed. The true lover is ever slow to believe in himself or his own chances, and the advent of Grant, younger than he is by some years, and handsome, and earnest—so very evidently in earnest—has damped his spirits. Up to this, ever since her illness, Nell has seemed so altogether his own that he can scarcely bear now to see another come in to divide his honours with him. It was nothing to him that the girl had refused cake from Grant, and had accepted bread and butter from him, though if he had heart to remember, he might have consoled himself with the recollection, that Nell is as fond of a cake as a child of five.

But Grant had come, looking so handsome, so brilliant, and the girl had received him with such sweet cordiality as seemed to Wortley but the continuation of a love begun in happier days.

Besides being modest, the true lover is always a little stupid. And Wortley's stupidity goes so far, that even now when Grant has gone—escorted to the gate by Cecilia and Gaveston, who quite understand his state of mind and are truly sorry for him —he cannot see that Nell is in a way relieved, and glad of his departure. The fact that this relief takes the form of silence, perhaps adds to his mystification.

For a long time he does not speak, and then at last—seeing that neither Cecilia nor Gaveston mean returning, and that the night air is drawing near with a chill within its train, he so far rouses himself as to say gruffly:

"It is growing too late for you to be out here. You must come in."

"Yes. I think so," says Nell. She gets up from her cushions, always so carefully arranged for her upon her garden chair, and with the help of her stick takes a step forward, then she catches hold of the arm of the chair, laughing softly, if a little nervously.

"My feet don't seem quite my own yet," says she, "I have sat here too long, perhaps. And this stick is no good—you must give me your arm, I'm afraid."

"You have sat out here far too long," growls he. "I don't know how they let you do it. As for that stick——"

He puts it aside in a masterful way, and taking her up in his arms, carries her—as he has so often done before in her hopeless days—through the open window, into the drawing room.

Here he lets her go, slowly, until her feet touch the carpet, and even then . . . it seems so *hard* to let her go!

All at once, as she feels his arms loosen,

they tighten round her again, and she knows that he is straining her passionately to his breast.

"*How* can I let you go?" says he. His tone sounds suffocated. "But I'll have to. I know it. I knew it this evening when he came again. There, don't mind me."

He releases her, and would have pressed her tenderly into a lounging chair near, but she, closing her slender fingers on the sleeve of his coat, prevents him. Leaning back from him, she looks up into his face, and he looks down at her, with his strong, kind, rather ugly face, very white and set.

There is a long, long pause, and then at last:

"*Don't* let me go!" says she.

She almost pushes him from her when the dreadful words are said, and I think she would have fallen but that he catches her and holds her.

"Nell!"

His voice is trembling, his heart beating with an almost cruel haste. He is bending over her, pressing his cheek against the pretty head now lying on his breast.

"Nellie!" says he again. But she is crying nervously now, and it is quite a minute or so before she can be got to speak. And then her abasement knows no depths.

"Oh, yes, I know. No wonder you are shocked! as you *are*—as you *must* be! It—it was a proposal. Oh! I don't know *how* I did it!"

There are several intervals that need not be recorded, as all true lovers can fill them in for themselves, and presently she grows comforted, and a little gleam of her old self steals forth.

"It *was* a proposal, for all you may say," says she. But the pretty saucy smile breaks out here, and there is a twinkle in the dewy eyes that argues considerable life for him in the coming days, "I hope you are not going to—*refuse me!*"

* * * * *

An hour later they are still as full of conversation as though the day had just begun. Truly, the genius of lovers is wonderful.

"I shall take you abroad myself. No one

could look after you as I could. We'll speak to Cecilia."

He had never called Mrs. Gaveston Cecilia until this moment, but already he regards her as a sister.

" Yes; and really after all, I don't want a nurse any more."

" Even if you did, I'd be your nurse."

At this they both laugh.

" A nice nurse *you'd* be," says Nell. Then all at once her mood changes, and she looks up at him with anxious eyes. " Do you remember now how you used to scold me—to find fault with me ?—I'm just the same now, you know, as I was then."

" That is what I like to think," says he.

" Is it?" She pauses, as if meditating upon this. " You," after a bit, " thought me troublesome ! "

" I like that thought too. The more troublesome you are, the more I shall have to do for you."

" There was one day when you said——"

But she never gets to the end of that sentence.

"Look here," says he, "I won't have all my crimes brought up against me like this. It's beastly unfair—that's what *I* call it—and after all you ought to be generous over my faults, because it was pure despair of ever gaining you that drove me to the brutalities you mention."

He laughs—but she does not—and after a moment she leans towards him, and pulls him to her with both hands.

"You do love me then? You *do*?" asks she.

There is so much honest doubt in her voice that it shocks him. Can't she *see*?

"My darling——"

"No, no, no," pushing him away. "As you," vehemently, "never *have* loved, and never *could* love anyone again?"

"I thought it was plain, my sweetheart," says he reproachfully. "But there is this, Nell, that all the world and everything in it, is of no account to me, except you, and *your* love for me, and *my* love for you!"

THE END.

www.ingramcontent.com/pod-product-compliance
Lightning Source LLC
Chambersburg PA
CBHW031735230426
43669CB00007B/350